The Cambridge Manuals of Science and
Literature

T0352051

THE CIVILIZATION OF ANCIENT
MEXICO

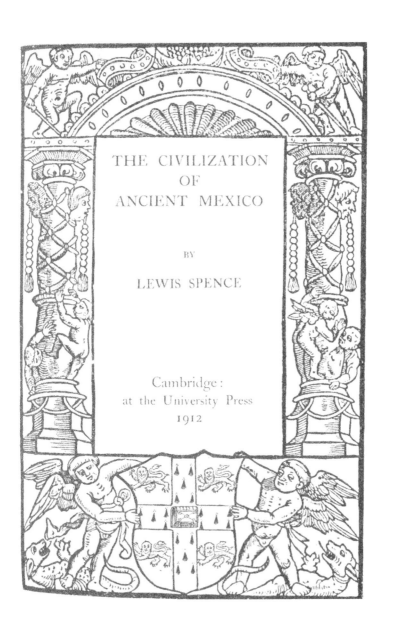

THE CIVILIZATION
OF
ANCIENT MEXICO

BY

LEWIS SPENCE

Cambridge:
at the University Press
1912

CAMBRIDGE UNIVERSITY PRESS
Cambridge, New York, Melbourne, Madrid, Cape Town,
Singapore, São Paulo, Delhi, Tokyo, Mexico City

Cambridge University Press
The Edinburgh Building, Cambridge CB2 8RU, UK

Published in the United States of America by Cambridge University Press, New York

www.cambridge.org
Information on this title: www.cambridge.org/9781107605732

© Cambridge University Press 1912

First published 1912
First paperback edition 2011

A catalogue record for this publication is available from the British Library

ISBN 978-1-107-60573-2 Paperback

*With the exception of the coat of arms at
the foot, the design on the title page is a
reproduction of one used by the earliest known
Cambridge printer, John Siberch, 1521*

PREFACE

THE desire on the part of investigators to be comprehensive has proved the curse of American Aboriginal History. The false point of view which regarded the entire American continent as one area, the historical facts concerning which might be included in one work—no matter how large—has been accountable for some dozens of "Histories of America," "Histories of the Civilised Peoples of America," and suchlike bibliographical monstrosities, which, however much they may reflect credit upon the powers of endurance of their several authors exhibit only too pitifully the very human failings of that type of scholarship which wishes to be regarded as omniscient and encyclopædic.

But while the histories of the peoples of the New World have suffered from this tendency on the part of historians towards too great a comprehensiveness, it would be wrong to say that specialisation had accomplished nothing. Much ground has been gained, and many rough places have been made smooth. But unfortunately the best part of this work has been issued in pamphlet form and in the transactions of various learned societies—a method of publication disastrous to the popularity of any subject.

Since the time of Prescott no attempt appears to have been made to collate and present within reasonable compass for popular consumption the vast amount of matter, ancient and modern, relating to the history of the Mexican people. The author does not claim to have done this. Others have attempted it, but have usually presented it with their considerations upon other American civilizations. The purpose of this book is to provide not only a merely popular history of Ancient Mexico, but such a sketch of the subject as will appeal to serious students who may wish to adopt the study of Mexican antiquities. In its scope nothing has been included which is not strictly verifiable from original sources. Speculation has not been altogether abandoned, but has been omitted except in those instances where reasons of special import called for it. At the same time whilst doubtful matter has been almost ruthlessly eliminated, such traditions as appeared to possess any substratum of fact and value from their bearing upon Mexican history, have not been altogether ignored, but have been included in the chapter upon the history of the Nahuan peoples, care being taken to draw particular attention to their legendary origin.

Mexican history must not be treated as other histories, but as a series of unembellished facts. Too little is known regarding it to permit us to indulge in speculation regarding the political relations of the peoples of Anahuac with one another, and this must be left undone until archæological research has supplied us with more extended data upon which to found such theories. To treat Nahuan history as we might that of any European country is absurd in the face of an unparalleled dearth of original documentary sources.

In conclusion, if this book introduces a section of the reading public to a new and fascinating study, I will feel that my labours in connection with it have been amply repaid.

LEWIS SPENCE.

Sept., 1912.

CONTENTS

LIST OF ILLUSTRATIONS

Figs. 6 and 7 are reproduced from the *Encyclopaedia Britannica* (eleventh edition).

CHAPTER I

INTRODUCTORY

Introduction — Mexico, its Physical Geography — Aboriginal Peoples — The Nahua Race — Their Language — Original Home.

THE study of the civilisations of ancient Mexico and Central America is fraught with much more importance than would at first sight appear, as from the consideration of the histories of these communities we are enabled to trace the almost complete evolution of a race, absolutely isolated from the rest of mankind, through the various stages of savagery and barbarism to one of comparative advancement in the scale of human existence. Apart from its merely historical importance the subject must ever possess a deeply romantic interest from the very circumstances under which the race, whose antiquities we are about to examine, was isolated by the lapse of ages from the rest of the human family. The origin of these civilised peoples, their possible affinities with the various European and Asiatic races, and the method by which they succeeded in reaching the new-found continent, were questions which agitated the scholars of Europe for many generations subsequent to the discovery of America, and if these problems do not appear so obscure as they once did, because of the labours recently lavished upon them by a band of able though widely dispersed scholars, they have at least lost none of the intense interest which must ever attach to them.

The area covered by the ancient Nahuan or Mexican race, both in its fluctuant and settled conditions, extended in its utmost limits from British Columbia in the north to Costa Rica in the south, the principal theatre of the race being confined, however, to the Mexican plateau proper and its immediate vicinity, that is from the boundaries of Texas and New Mexico on the north to the Isthmus of Tehuantepec on the south. This plateau, which was known to them as Anahuac[1], is 69,000 square miles in extent, and from 6,000 to 8,500 feet above sea-level, including in its gradual elevation from the sea-coast all varieties of temperature, from the torrid heat of the tropics to a genial climate analogous to that of Italy. This elevation is formed by the mountain range of the Mexican Cordilleras which, near their highest point, the peak of Orizaba, divide

---

[1] "Near the water." The original allusion was to the vicinity of the lakes.

into an eastern and a western range. Between these twin mountain systems lies the plateau of Anahuac the land of the Nahua proper, as distinguished from kindred, aboriginal, or conquered peoples. This plateau is formed by the ridges of the mountains of the bifurcated system alluded to, the peaks of which rise from 14,000 to 17,000 feet above sea-level. This table-land, which has many deep and warmer valleys, gradually expands in breadth as it extends to the north, and remains at an average elevation of about 6,000 feet above sea-level as far as 420 miles from the city of Mexico, after which it gradually declines.

The races which inhabited Mexico before the coming of the Nahua were many and diverse. Commencing at the southern extremity of the country we find the Huaxteca, a Maya-speaking people, who had long been settled about Tampico on the Mexican Gulf. The Mexicans named their territory Huaxtlan, or land of the tamarind, which grew there abundantly. To the northward of Vera Cruz on the Mexican Gulf dwelt the Totonacs, and at the estuary of the Tabasco river the Chontals. On the Pacific shore southward of Mexico the Mixtecâ and the Zapotecâ adjoined each other, while a tract of considerable dimensions was inhabited by the Tarascâ, who occupied a part of the modern province of Michoacan. The Cohuixcans also dwelt on the Pacific side. But the most

important aboriginal population of Mexico was that
of the Otomi, who still occupy the plateau of the
Guanajuato and Queretaro, and who, before the
advent of the Nahua races, probably peopled the
entire Mexican plateau. Their language is of the
type known as "incorporative," that is, one word
embraces several, and appears to have some affinity
to the Athapascan dialect of British North America[1].
It is probable, however, that these several peoples
were themselves newcomers in the land. The
Totonacs and Chontals were in all likelihood allied
to tribes dwelling to the south-east of the Yucatan
peninsula who spoke a similar language, and their
migration to the lands they occupied was possibly
effected from south to north by way of the Mexican
Gulf. The Tarascâ claimed to be of the same stock
as the Nahua, but their language and characteristics
render this extremely doubtful. Here and there
among the more secluded valleys are still found
communities which probably represent a yet more
archaic people. These are the Popolcan, Mixe,
Chinantec, Zoque, Mazatec, Cuicatec, Chocho, and
Mazahua, the latter allied.to the Otomi.

The Ulmecs "People of the Rubber Land," and
Xicalancans "People of the Land of Pumpkins," were
also early settlers, and probably came from the Tierra
Caliente or hot country near the eastern coasts of

[1] D. G. Brinton, *Myths of the New World*, p. 38.

Mexico, while the Nonohualco dwelt at the southern end of the Lake of Chalco.

The Nahua peoples included all those tribes and confederacies speaking the Mexican language or Nahuatlatolli, and designated themselves "Nahuatlacâ," a term signifying "those who live in accordance with a settled rule of life." They appear to have extended in their geographical distribution, at various periods, from British Columbia on the north to the Isthmus of Tehuantepec on the south.

The Nahuan tongue, or Nahuatlatolli, was the language of a barbarism little removed from savagery, representing a low state of mental culture. It must be borne in mind that the Aztecâ, from whom we get our ideas of the Nahuan tongue, on their entrance to Anahuac (as they designated the Mexican plateau), were in a condition akin to mere savagery, and that they were simply the heirs of an older civilisation. The people who possessed this older culture were much more polished, and probably spoke a more cultivated dialect of the same tongue. If they did so, it is for ever lost to us. Like most other American languages Mexican belongs to the incorporative type. In all languages, every grammatical sentence conveys one leading idea, and "incorporative" language "seeks to unite in the most intimate manner all relations and modifications with the leading idea, to merge one in the other by altering

the forms of the words themselves, and, welding them
together to express the whole in one word, and to
banish any conception except as it arises in relation
to others[1]."

Much difference of opinion exists as to the locality
where the Nahua People originated or gained those
characteristics and formed that language which
entitles them to be regarded as a separate branch
of the American Race. Those theories which would
seek for them a southern origin may be summarily
dismissed, as linguistic and ethnological research has
discovered affinities between the Nahuatlatolli and the
tongues of existing northern peoples, notably to the
Tsimshian Nootka-Columbian group, including the
Wakash, Ahts, Haidah, and Quaquiutl, all inhabiting
British Columbia. This resemblance, however, is
most marked as regards religious conceptions and
artistic efforts. The early beliefs of the Nahua
peoples centred round the worship of Quetzalcoatl,
the Man of the Sun (see p. 58), who descended
from the sun in the form of a bird, and resumed his
human shape in order to instruct mankind in the arts
of civilisation. This deity the Thlingit recognise as
"Yetl," the Quaquiutl as "Kanikilak," the Salish of
the coast as "Kumsnöotl," "Quäaqa," or "Släalekam[2]."

[1] Brinton, *Myths of the New World*, p. 19.

[2] *Brit. Assoc. 5th Rep. of the Committee on the N.W. Tribes of the
Dominion of Canada*, 1889, pp. 29–51.

The resemblance between British Columbian art-forms and those of the Nahua is too striking to be accounted for in any other way than by a common origin[1]. This applies especially to the art of sculpture, in which these northern tribes have acquired an unique and curious style. Marchand in his *Voyages* (Tom. II. p. 282) is so struck with this resemblance that he argues that the Haidah Indians must have arrived at their present seat from Mexico or Central America, and the substantial identity of the idol forms of Mexico with those still found in the Haidah lodges it is not possible to doubt, according to Payne (*op. cit.* Vol. II. p. 377). Nor is the advancement of these northern tribes of recent origin. Every circumstance indicates its remote antiquity, and a trustworthy investigator has remarked upon the prolonged isolation necessary for its development[2]. The traditions of the Nahua as to the place of their origin would also appear to strongly fortify the theory that they first became a homogeneous racial family in the district of British Columbia. They universally described their ancestors as immigrants from the north, who had reached the Mexican plateau in successive swarms, by way of Xalisco, or the "Land of Sand." The name "Aztlan," so often met with in the writings of the Spanish historians of ancient

---

[1] Payne, *Hist. of the New World called America*, Vol. II. pp. 376–7.
[2] Boas, *Bull. Amer. Geo. Soc.*, Vol. XXXIII. p. 229.

Mexico as the place of origin of the Aztecâ, is of
doubtful value as a genuine remnant of ancient
tradition, but "Tlapallan" and "Chicomoztoc" or
"the Seven Caves," may represent Arizona or New
Mexico. It is wholly unlikely that the Nahua
swarmed into Mexico directly from British Columbia,
and their traditions describe many stopping-places
on the way where their forefathers sojourned for
periods of longer or shorter duration[1].

CHAPTER II

THE MEXICAN PEOPLES

Probable Route of the Nahua Migration—The Toltec Question—
The Chichimecâ—The Aculhuaque—The Tecpanecs—The
Aztecâ—Other Races of the Mexican Plateau.

NAHUA legend which deals with the migrations of
the race states that they had long dwelt in "Tlapallan,"
or "the Place of Bright Colours," described as a
maritime country, which they reached by sea, coasting
southwards along the shore of California. There is
every reason to believe that their migrations took
place by land, following the valleys and plains of the
Rocky Mountains; yet there is a possibility that bodies

[1] *Vide* Chap. II.

of the Nahua reached Mexico by canoe. There is no reason to doubt that the British Columbian tribes were early maritime adventurers; and the native god Quetzalcoatl is represented as being a skilful manager of the canoe, and as riding on a sea-monster[1].

The Toltecs, the first Nahuan immigrants, says Ixtlilxochitl[2], the Texcucan chronicler, after their arrival from Chicomoztoc in the maritime country of Tlapallan or Huehuetlapallan, passed the country of Xalisco, and landed at the port of Huatulco, travelled by land until they reached Tochtepec or Tototepec on the Pacific coast, and from that spot worked their way inland to Tollantzinco. This migration, states the legend, occupied 104 years. "This account," says Payne, "undoubtedly exhibits a remarkable coincidence with the ethno-geographical facts distinguishing the coast alleged to have been passed along"; but he proceeds to state that in his opinion it was invented to account for the distribution of the language, or at least adapted to it, as "it seems incredible that an ethno-geographical distribution should to this day exist substantially unaltered which was effected by a migration alleged to have taken place before the foundation of Tollan[3]." Another legend of the Toltec migration agrees with the first in stating that Tlapallan, the northernmost station of

---

[1] Dresden Codex, pp. 25–45.	[2] *Hist. Chichimeca.*
[3] *Hist. of the New World called America*, Vol. II. p. 420.

the immigrants, had been reached by coasting along
the Californian shore, but differs as to the halting-
places mentioned on the route.　The most probable
route taken by an immigrant tribe would appear
to be directly south-eastwards over the plains of
Chihuahua, Durango, and Zacatecas, until the plateau
of Anahuac was reached, when they would descend to
the Mexican Gulf in the east, and the Pacific shore in
the west.

　　The question relative to the origin and identity of
the Toltec race who are supposed at some distant
period to have inhabited the plateau of Anahuac
bristles with difficulties.　Some authorities allow to
them a merely legendary status ; others insist that they
were a semi-legendary race analogous to the Picts of
Scottish history ; whilst still others claim for them
the full acknowledgment of a people with an undoubted historical position.　These rival hypotheses
we will briefly describe and sift :—(1) the legendary
evidence as to their origin and history ; (2) the theory
of modern authorities that they existed solely as
a figment of Nahua mythology ; and (3) hypotheses
regarding their historicity and authentic existence.

　　(1)　Legends relating to the Toltec migrations
have already been described and examined.　In the
Nahua mind the Toltecs were a people of cognate
race to the Nahua themselves, and speaking the
same language, who had either perished or been

driven from the Mexican plateau by various dis-
turbing causes. They had, according to tradition,
possessed a civilisation of a high standard and great
complexity, which was supposed to have formed the
basis of all subsequent Nahua civilisations. Their
principal territory was in Tollan, a city lying north-
west of the mountains which bound the Mexican
valley, and built near a small river whose waters flow
into the Mexican Gulf. Their religion centred around
the figure of Quetzalcoatl, a deity whose attributes
are fully described in chapter VI of the present
volume. They possessed a sacred book named the
Teoamoxtli; in which the tenets of laws, religion,
and medicine were supposed to be set forth—as
Prescott sagely remarks, "a good deal too much
for one book."

The chief authority for the legendary description
of the Toltecs is the *Relaciones* of the half-caste
Indian historian, Don Fernando de Alva Ixtlilxochitl,
which gives the date at which they settled in Anahuac
as the beginning of the sixth century, and that of the
fall of their empire as 1055. However he gives
conflicting details concerning them in two different
places, and is obviously untrustworthy.

(2)   The theory that the Toltecs were a mythical
people has some authority behind it, but breaks
down upon a close examination of other criteria. It
is partly based upon a supposed decree that the

rule of each individual monarch should last neither
more nor less that fifty-two years. This was the
period of the great Mexican cycle of years, which was
adopted so that the ritual calendar might coincide
with the solar year—certainly a most suspicious
coincidence. Furthermore many names in the Toltec
dynasty correspond with the names of gods, and
give the list a hypothetical value. Dr Brinton has
alluded to the Toltecs as "children of the sun," and
sees in them merely the offspring of the great
luminary who, as in Peruvian myth, sent his children
to civilise the human race. This theory is strengthened by the fact that Quetzalcoatl, the Man of the
Sun, is King of the Toltecs[1].

(3) Payne, with others, will not have it that the
Toltecs are mythical, but sees in them a veritable
people of history. "There can be no doubt," he says,
"that the accounts of Toltec history current at the
Conquest contain a nucleus of substantial truth[2]";
and again "To doubt that there once existed in Tollan
an advancement superior to that which prevailed
among the Nahuatlacâ generally at the Conquest,
and that its people spread this advancement throughout Anahuac and into the districts eastward and
southward, would be to reject a belief universally

---

[1] See also Fórstemann's *Theory of the Toltecs*, Bull. 28, B. A. E.,
p. 541.
[2] *Hist. of the New World called America*, Vol. II. p. 417.

entertained and confirmed, rather than shaken, by the efforts made in later times to construct for the pueblo something in the nature of a history[1]."

It may then be briefly laid down regarding the Toltecs :—

(1) That a most persistent body of tradition as to their existence gained credence among the Nahua ;

(2) That the date (1055) of their alleged dispersal permits of the approximate exactness and probability of this body of tradition at the time of the Conquest ;

(3) That the site of Tollan contains ruins of a description more archaic than the architecture of the Nahua ; and

(4) That the early Nahua having, within their own recollection, existed as savage tribes, the time which elapsed between the primitive and the advanced stages of their civilisation was too short to admit of the evolution from one to the other. Hence their adoption of an older Mexican civilisation must be presupposed.

The above facts would thus appear to indicate that the Toltecs actually existed as a people. But little more can be said of them. The vast amount of legendary matter which has collected around the name of Toltec is for the most part absolutely futile,

---

[1] *Hist. of the New World called America*, Vol. II. p. 430.

and the mere fact that they existed must be sufficient for us. There is also not a shred of satisfactory evidence that they settled in any portion of Central America, as Payne and others seem to think. Many writers imagine that the Toltecs were the founders of the civilisation of Central America, but evidence is lacking to prove this. Such documents and authorities as pretend to give an account of their State will be examined in the chapter dealing with the history of the Nahua.

The Chichimecâ, or Chichimecs, were probably of Otomi origin (see p. 4), and were supposed to have entered the valley of Anahuac subsequently to the Toltecs, where they built the towns of Tenayucan and Texcuco, and formed an alliance with Tollantzinco. Later they colonised Texcuco from Tenayucan, and about the close of the thirteenth century the Chichimec headquarters were removed thither. Here they afterwards came into the sphere of Nahuan influence, and under the leadership of Nahua over-lords founded a great confederacy, which rivalled that of the Tecpanecs on the opposite shore of the lake of Texcuco. They subsequently mingled much with Nahua elements, and their culture, and even their speech, became Nahuan. Indeed it is question-able whether the Chichimecâ had not been a loosely combined federation of several races ere they entered Mexico. The names of the principal

Chichimec tribes are given by José de Acosta in his *Historia Natural y Moral de las Yndias* (Seville, 1580), as Pames, Otomes, Pintos, Michoacacques, and Tarascos. Nearly all these tribes were of aboriginal origin, and, to sum up, the Chichimecs may be regarded as of Otomi race *plus* other aboriginal elements *plus* later Nahua elements. Other pueblos or towns founded or inhabited by the Chichimecâ were Xochimilco, Xaltocan, Otumpan, and Teotihuacan.

The Aculhuaque were the first authenticated Nahua immigrants to the Valley of Mexico. The name implies "Strong" or "Tall Men." In his *Conquista de Mexico* Gomara states that they arrived in the neighbourhood of Mexico from Aculhuacan, their previous dwelling-place, about 780 A.D., and established the pueblos or settlements of Tollantzinco, Tollan, Cohualtichan, and Culhuacan, and laid the foundations of Mexico. These immigrants spread from Tollantzinco, their first settlement in the north of the valley, and from thence one of their branches turned westward and settled at Tollan, the other proceeding southwards to the Mexican Valley, and the districts of Tlaxcallan, Cholula, and Huexotzinco. Of these pueblos, the most important was Tlaxcallan, or Tlascala, the inveterate foe of the Aztecâ. (See Chapter v.)

The Tecpanecs were a confederation of Nahua pueblos inhabiting the lower margin of the Lake of

Texcuco, in the vicinity of Culhuacan, the principal of which were Azcapozalco, Tlacopan, Coyohuacan, Atlaquihuapan, and Huitzilopocho.   Gomara (*loc. cit.*) mentions a tradition which attributes the Tecpanec settlements to a separate Nahuan migration which occurred long after the founding of Culhuacan. In this division of the Nahua were evolved those institutions which came to be regarded as typical of the race, especially in Texcuco and Mexico.   It is not certain that the name Tecpanec has any specific value as a racial description, the word simply signifying that each settlement possessed its own *tecpan* or chief's house.   This confederation was the great rival to the Chichimec-Otomi confederacy.

The Aztecâ or Aztecs were a wandering tribe of doubtful extraction, but probably of Nahuan origin, who had roamed from place to place on the Mexican plateau, at length settling in those marshy lands which had been left bare by the retreating waters of the Lake of Texcuco, near Tlacopan and Azcapozalco. They received their name, which means " Crane People," from the Tecpanecs, probably because of their marsh-dwelling habits in which they resembled the bird whose name they received, or, perhaps, because they came from a district in the north called Aztlan or "Crane Land," probably Chihuahua.   According to their own account they had left this country in the latter half of the twelfth century, and had probably attached themselves to, or followed after some branch of the Aculhuaque, whom they accompanied into the Mexican valley. The places at which they sojourned temporarily were Hueyculhua-can, Tzompanco, Ehecatepec, and Tepeyacac, and they made prolonged residences at Culhuacan, Chapultepec, and, finally, the marshes of the Mexican lake, where they paid tribute to the Tecpanec chiefs, to whom they became auxiliaries. They founded the pueblos of Tenochtitlan and Tlatelalco, and about the middle of the fourteenth century had become powerful allies to the Tecpanecs.

The numerous cognate peoples who had settled to the north and south of the table-land of Mexico were almost unknown to the central confederacies, whose ethnology we have been examining. The Zapotecs, Mixtecs, and Kuikatecs of the south—all non-Nahuan —were under the cultured influence of the Mayas of Central America. The Kuikatecs wandered for nearly six hundred years in the borderland between the Nahua and Maya ere they settled in Acolan, and the Zapotecs invaded the Maya territory itself. The Zapotecs finally settled in the district which is the modern Mexican province of Oaxaca.

CHAPTER III

EARLY HISTORY OF THE MEXICAN PEOPLE

The Sources of Mexican History—The Pinturas—The Histories
written by Civilised Natives—The Spanish Historians.

In the study of Mexican history it must ever be
borne in mind that it is the history of those Mexican
communities alone which chanced to be in a flourishing
condition at the period of the Conquest concerning
which we have any definite accounts. Of those
states which preceded the kingdoms which occupied
a prominent position on the arrival of Cortez we are
almost totally ignorant. The history of Mexico is
a history of communities, not of one homogeneous
nation. Each city possessed its own king, government,
and territory, and was self-dependent. Indeed the
political condition of the Mexican plateau forcibly
reminds us of that of early Palestine, where each
community was independent of the rest.

The first source of Mexican history to which
attention must be directed is found in those "pinturas"
or paintings by which the various Mexican states kept
their chronological records. In the greater states these
records were often exceedingly full of detail, indicating the incidence of festivals, sacrifices, tributes,

and the general annual round of the life of the people.
The " Nexiuhilpilitztli " or " sheaf of fifty-two years "
(p. 92) was also reckoned by the larger states, and
natural phenomena, such as floods, eclipses, and un-
usual events of all descriptions, were also noted, as
were, of course, the accession and demise of kings.
This collection of what may be regarded as indis-
putable facts was embodied in painted representations
of the events detailed by native artists who were
trained from youth in the execution of emblematic
draughtsmanship.　　They were depicted in bright
and unmistakeable colours with a brush of feathers
on parchments, paper, or rolls of cotton or cloth
manufactured from the fibre of the aloe (p. 107),
and were usually painted upon both sides.　　These
records were folded and the ends covered by boards.
They were interpreted by *amamatini*, or " readers "
who had learned by heart the " story " they told, and
in reality they were only a mnemonic aid to the
traditional histories of the several pueblos.　　It was
upon these paintings, together with the traditional
lore which accompanied them, that the early Spanish
historians relied for the basis of their histories of the
Mexican people.

The majority of these manuscripts have been
destroyed, either by the fanaticism of the Spanish
conquerors, or by the still more powerful depredations
of time.　　The more enlightened *literati* of Europe

regarded this wholesale destruction as lamentable, and took steps to have copies of the more important pinturas made by such executants of the art as still survived, and to have added to them interpretations taken *viva voce* from the native readers themselves. These, which are known as Interpretative Codices, are of considerable value in the elucidation of Mexican history and life, and three are still preserved. These three codices have but little in common. The Vatican manuscripts deal specially with Mexican mythology and the calendar. The Paris or Telleriano-Remensis Codex gives some details regarding the early settlement of the various pueblos, and, with the Oxford Codex, furnishes a historical chronicle which is lacking in the Vatican Codex. The Oxford Codex is chiefly remarkable, however, for the full list it gives of those pueblos which were in a state of vassalage to Mexico, with their tributes, and, on the whole, considering the other details furnished by it, it must be regarded as the most important of the three as an aid to the elucidation of the history of the Mexican people.

It will readily be recognised that such pinturas as were recovered from the ruins of the Mexican civilisation, unaccompanied as they were by interpretations, are of considerably less importance to the student of Mexican history. They deal chiefly with ritual, astrology, and the various aspects of the

calendar, in the consideration of which was contained
all the lore of the Nahua, and one, the Vatican MS.
No. 3773, is a species of religious handbook, representing the journey after death through the underworld.

The labours of the early Spanish historians of
Mexico were supplemented by those of several
authors of native or semi-Indian blood. One of
the principal of these was Don Fernando de Alva
Ixtlilxochitl, a half-breed, of noble Texcucan descent,
who wrote two works entitled *Historia Chichimeca*,
or History of the Chichimecs, and *Relaciones*. In
both of these he attributes to the Texcucan and
Mexican communities a degree of civilisation and
splendour which must make us regard his whole
narrative with great suspicion.

The most trustworthy authority for Mexican
mythology is Fray Bernardino Sahagun, a Spanish
monk who came to Mexico in 1524, three years after
its conquest, and for many years laboured inde-
fatigably to collect the lore of the natives, with
especial reference to their religious customs. These
he embodied in an admirable work *Historia General
de las Cosas de Nueva España*, which, through
priestly opposition, was not published until 1829 in
Mexico. It is now regarded as the chief source of
our knowledge of Aztec customs and rites, and its
value lies in the fact that it consists of what is
practically first-hand evidence, its materials having

been collected from native sources. Torquemada's work, *Monarchia Indiana*, Seville, 1615, is to a great extent a paraphrase of Sahagun's, which was then unknown, but it is valuable for its manifest integrity, and the care with which its author has selected his sources. The Abbé Clavigero's *Storia Antica del Messico* (Cesena, 1780) was written with the object of clearing up the legendary mists which until his time had shrouded Mexican history, and many chronological inaccuracies and misstatements are corrected therein. These three historians will be found the most valuable to the student of Mexican antiquities. The others, such as Bernal Diaz, Camargo, Veytia, etc., are more confined to the condition of the country when they entered it, and are by no means trustworthy in regard to its antiquities.

CHAPTER IV

THE FOUNDATION OF ACOLHUAN PUEBLOS

THE adoption by the Nahua peoples of a settled mode of existence on an agricultural basis was probably a very gradual process. At the period of the entrance of their first immigrants on the Mexican plateau, it is clear that they were a people still in the hunter stage of existence, ignorant of any arts save those which pertain to a barbarous state of life, and with no desire to adopt a more settled condition[1]. Soon the nature of their environment began to influence their mode of life. They dwelt in a more genial climate than that of the land whence they had come. The maize plant had been introduced as a staple of diet in the territories which they entered long before their occupation of them. The lakes provided a plentiful supply of fish and esculent shell-fish. The soil produced abundant fruits without the necessity of tillage. In short their whole environment favoured the speedy adoption of a sedentary mode of existence.

In this new and more fertile land they did not, however, lose those bellicose characteristics for which they became afterwards notorious. Indeed the earliest traditions concerning them are of a war-like nature. They tell of prolonged struggles with a race of giants designated Quinames, of whom they enumerate four separate generations. These legends obviously relate to a period when the Nahua had a long and severe struggle with the aboriginal inhabitants of the country.

But few fragments exist, as we have before pointed out, which can give the Toltecs a position in veritable history. Torquemada claims to have seen certain

---

[1] José de Acosta, *Hist. Nat. y Mor. de las Yndias.* Seville, 1580.

ancient pinturas reputed to have been the work of Toltec artists[1]. He believed these to be genuine, and uses them as authentic authorities regarding the manufacture of cotton by the Toltecs. This however proves nothing. The various accounts of the Toltecs incorporated in the records of the more modern Mexican states, for instance in those of Culhuacan, Quauhtitlan, and Texcuco, appear to possess a sub-stratum of fact, how much exactly it would be difficult to say. Tradition has it that the Toltec capital, Tollan, stood upon the site of the modern city of Tula.

Shortly after its foundation Tollan reached a position of considerable importance. The Toltecs are referred to by the Spanish historians as being a race skilled in all the arts of civilisation and refine-ment. But it is not our intention in such a work as this to burden the student with a mass of legendary detail, with which he will become all too soon woe-fully familiar. Our object is to afford him a sketch of such historical facts concerning the Nahua peoples as is verifiable in the usual manner by reference to original sources.

The records of Culhuacan, Quauhtitlan, and Texcuco contain accounts of Toltec history which may be accepted for what they appear to be worth.

[1] *Monarchia Indiana*, Tom. I. p. 67.

The Culhuacan records contain a list of four Toltec rulers, grouped in pairs as follows :—

Totepiuh, Topiltzin,
Hueymactzin, Nauhyotzin.

The first pair, according to the Spanish historian Zumárraga, were the leaders of the first Nahuan swarm which founded Tollantzinco. That they are mythical is undoubted, as nearly a century elapses between them and the second pair. These appear to be equally shadowy, and the efforts of historians, ancient and modern, to prove them authentic seem anything but successful[1].

The annals of Quauhtitlan and Texcuco are no more convincing than those of Culhuacan. The former supplies a list of royal names, the lives of whose owners are asserted to have spread over four centuries. The fact that among these personages is the god Quetzalcoatl is sufficient to stamp the whole as purely fictitious. The Texcucan list exhibits many differences from that of Quauhtitlan, and is equally spurious, as the reign of each monarch is made to coincide with the duration of fifty-two years which completed a "sheaf of years," indicating the lapse of a well-marked chronological period in use among the Nahua.

With the name of Topiltzin, the last chief of

[1] Payne, *loc. cit.* Vol. II. pp. 426–7. Zumárraga, *Tezozomoc Cronica* (ed. Orozco y Berra), p. 183.

Tollan, is associated the legend of its fall. He is described as an illegitimate son of the preceding ruler, and consequent upon his accession to power a revolution took place, the results of which were destructive to the existence of Tollan. The dispersal of the Toltecs followed. They are said to have wandered eastwards to Campeachy, and also towards the south, and in them many historians have seen the founders of the civilisations of the various Central American states of the Maya peoples. The name "Tulan" certainly figures in the legends of the Maya. But it is used to designate any populous and magnificent royal city. Many difficulties exist regarding the identification of the Tollan of the Nahua with the four Mayan cities so named, the chief of which problems is that the Toltecs are invariably described as of Nahua race, and as speaking the same language, which differs radically from the Maya.

The traditions concerning the foundation of the earliest pueblos of the Aculhuaque state that they were almost contemporary with Tollan itself. Indeed their settlements of Tollantzinco (Tollan the Lesser) and Cholula are invariably associated with Tollan in the accounts of that state. Cholula is supposed to have been the inheritor of the culture of the Toltecs, and in later times was an ally of the confederacy which consisted of Mexico, Texcuco, and Tlacopan, but was in no wise subservient to these states. Tollantzinco is stated to have been early merged among the Chichimec states by a royal marriage, although from time to time its people attempted to assert their independence by an appeal to arms[1].

Cholula, the successor of the semi-mythical Tollan, certain of whose inhabitants sought safety there on the destruction of their own city, maintained an offensive and defensive alliance with the states of Tlaxcallan, or Tlascala, and Huexotzinco. These three pueblos were situated almost exactly where the mountain ranges encircling the Mexican plateau fork off from a common branch, having the peaks of Popocatepetl and Matlalcueye to the west and east respectively. The city of Cholula was the Mecca of the Mexicans, as being the headquarters of the god Quetzalcoatl, a sun-and-culture god, who may have been the especial deity of the Toltecs, and whose worship was somewhat dissimilar to that of any other Mexican god (see Chap. III.). It was famed for the work of its artists in the precious metals, and excavations upon its site have brought to light many objects of archaeological value.

[1] Torquemada, Vol. I. p. 66.

CHAPTER V

Tlaxcallan—The Valley Pueblos—Early Dominant States—The
Tecpanecs—Rise of Texcuco—The Aztecâ—Rise of New
Powers—The Last Kings of Mexico.

TLAXCALLAN, or Tlascala, situated some seven
leagues from Cholula, had been founded by the
Aculhuaque, or Acolhuans at a later date. It was in
reality a district containing four towns, Tepeticpac
(originally an Ulmec pueblo), Ocatelolco, Quiahuiztlan,
and Tizitlan, with some twenty-eight villages, the
entire territory occupying less than forty square miles,
with a probable population of about half a million.
The extreme isolation of this people had resulted in
an almost complete and mutual oblivion of the unity
of race with the other Nahua peoples. The products
of the more fruitful districts of Mexico were not
admitted to their markets, and they were later regarded as a race merely existing for the supply of
sacrificial victims for the altars of Mexico. Once a year
the Tlascaltecs and Mexicans met on a prearranged
battle-ground and engaged in combat, not with the
object of slaying one another, but for the purpose of
supplying victims for the altars of their respective
gods Camaxtli and Huitzilopochtli. In this un-
natural strife the slaying of an enemy was not
regarded as so meritorious a feat as his capture

alive for the purpose of sacrifice[1]. These formidable
Tlascaltec warriors wreaked a fearful revenge on their
ancient enemies of Mexico upon the coming of the
Spaniards, and it is doubtful if without their aid Cortez
would have been able to accomplish the Conquest of
Mexico.

The Tlascaltecs formed a body of tradition in
verse or rhythmic prose, which has been made use of
by Torquemada[2]. They designated themselves Teo-
Chichimecs. This did not imply that they were of
the Chichimec race, the word being latterly used
to mean simply "hunter" or "warrior," the prefix
"Teo" signifying that they regarded themselves as
Chichimecs of the Sun, or of a superior caste. According to these traditional poems, the Tlascaltecs,
upon their original separation from the other Aculhuan
tribes, sojourned either near Texcuco or Poyauhtlan ;
but some accounts state that their original settlement
was the town of Cohuatlichan. Here their barbaric
and warlike habits so enraged the surrounding states
of Culhuacan, Azcapozalco, and Tenayucan that they
drove the Tlascaltecs from Cohuatlichan. The tribe
then divided into two bodies, one of which journeyed
northwards, halting at Tollantzinco, and proceeding to
the more isolated district of the Tierra Caliente, where
they founded Nahuatlan, Achachalintlan, Papantla,

---

[1] Muñoz-Camargo, *Historia de Tlascala* (A. Chavero, ed. 1892).
[2] *Monarchia Indiana.*

and other pueblos. The second division, travelling
south-eastward, settled round the slope of the great
volcano of Popocatepetl, but some of this number
entered the district of Tlaxcallan, then occupied by the
Ulmecs, whom they speedily subdued, and, spreading
rapidly southwards, they founded the pueblos of
Xalpan and Xichochimalco. The neighbouring people
of Huexotzinco became alarmed at the increase of
Tlascaltec dominion and drove the invaders to the
mountains. The Tlascaltecs sought the aid of
Texcuco, the Huexotzincans that of Azcapozalco.
The former were successful in the campaign which
ensued, and the Tecpanecs of Huexotzinco withdrew
with a higher opinion of the prowess of the Tlascaltecs[1]. These events are assigned by Chavero
(*loc. cit.*) to the year 1384.

The Tlascaltec dominion was now assured in its
own especial territory, and its prosperity attracted
a colony of Cholulans, who founded the quarter of
Tecuitlixco, and seized Ocotelolco, the most powerful
of the four Tlascaltec pueblos, represented by the
present town of Tlascala. The other settlements
of the Acolhuans in the plateau scarcely possess
a history. Huexotzinco is barely mentioned by
the Spanish historians. Regarding Tepeyacac and
Teohuacan they are likewise almost silent.

[1] Torquemada, Vol. i. p. 268, citing the epic poems of the
Tlascaltec bard Tequanitzin.

The centre of interest now shifts to the valley of Mexico, and to the pueblos grouped round the lakes of Tzumpanco, Xaltocan, Xochimilco, Texcuco, and Chalco (see map). These settlements numbered about fifty at the period of the Spanish Conquest, the most important of them being the states which surrounded the Lake of Texcuco. They had early acquired commercial importance through fostering the industry of salt refining, procuring the mineral from the lake by which they dwelt, and bartering it with the natives of other pueblos, who employed it in the preserving of flesh, and used it with their food. These lacustrine settlements grouped themselves round the rival states of Azcapozalco on the western side of the lake, and Texcuco on its eastern shores, and a fierce competition between these nuclei ended in the defeat of the former by its subservient pueblos, about a century before the advent of the Spanish Conquerors. The settlements which thus overthrew Azcapozalco attached themselves to Texcuco and its ally Tlacopan, and ultimately overran the entire territory of Mexico from the Mexican Gulf to the Pacific, with the exception of the hostile and necessarily boycotted districts of Tlaxcallan or Tlascala, the people of which existed solely for the provision of Mexican sacrifices, the "holy city" of Cholula, and the pueblo of Huexotzinco.

Texcuco, or Tezcuco may be regarded as of Otomi

origin, but had probably adopted the customs of the
Nahua before its rise to power, though it had not
altogether received their language, being in all likelihood bilingual in the Otomi and Nahua tongues.
But other confederacies had assisted in its rise to
power.   Two of the earliest pueblos, according to the
Paris Codex—Xaltocan and Tenayucan—were of
Otomi origin, and another, Culhuacan, was sup-
posedly of Toltec foundation.   Between these three
pueblos the territory of the valley would appear to
have been divided at a very early date.   The state of
Xaltocan is sometimes mentioned as having domi-
nated a territory embracing nearly the entire Mexican
Valley.   It was situated at the northern extremity of
the lake, and undoubtedly spread its influence to the
communities verging upon the southern waters.   But
there is little probability that its dominion extended
much farther.   The same may be said of Tenayucan,
situated on the north-western shores of the lake,
from which the Otomi Texcucans originally hailed.
There are traditions of its supremacy over the Tecpanecs, whose history is about to be dealt with, but
the probabilities are that its inhabitants evacuated
their ancient seat and founded Texcuco to escape the
rapidly-spreading Tecpanec dominion.   Of Culhuacan
the very geographical position is unknown.

With the arrival of the Tecpanec pueblos at a
position of importance the real history of the Mexican

Valley commences. Before the downfall of Culhuacan, these communities had been founded in its immediate vicinity. The more important were Azcapozalco, Tlacopan, Atlaquihuayan, Coyohuacan, and Huitzilo-pocho. The Tecpanecs were typical Nahua, but the name indicates no racial characteristic, merely signi-fying that each community possessed a *tecpan*, a "chief's house," or nucleus. The native records of Azcapozalco were said to carry back the history of that pueblo for 1561 years. But Torquemada is exceedingly sceptical of this extended chronology, and at a comparatively recent date its site must have been covered by the waters of the Lake of Texcuco. The fourteenth of those chiefs who figured in its chronicles was in power at the time of the Conquest, which would refer its history to a period no more distant than the twelfth century. Its northerly position gave it pre-eminence among the Tecpanec towns, as being the vanguard against the Otomi con-federacy to the north.

The Otomi people of Tenayucan had forsaken their town owing to the growing power of the Tec-panec pueblos on the western side of the lake, and at the end of the thirteenth century had migrated to its eastern shores, where they founded the pueblo of Texcuco. This change was effected by Quinantzin, the fourth chief in succession, and Texcuco rapidly grew in power and importance. A circumstance

occurred, however, which considerably altered its
racial complexion. The Tecpanec town of Culhuacan
having lost its importance, a large proportion of its
inhabitants crossed the lake to settle at Texcuco, and
were reinforced by Nahua people from other quarters,
so that Texcuco in a short period became almost
a Nahua city, and its population adopted the Nahua
tongue and customs. A cluster of new pueblos rose
around it, and, at the end of the fourteenth century,
the Tecpanec towns saw themselves confronted by a
confederacy numbering amongst its units Huexotlan,
Cohuatlichan, Acolman, and many lesser pueblos,
under the chieftainship of Techotlalatzin, the son of
the chief who had founded Texcuco.

The Tecpanecs, thus menaced by the new confederacy which had so rapidly arisen on the opposite
shore of the lake, received at this time a much-
needed accession to their forces. This was the Aztecâ
or "Crane People," who came from Aztlan or "Crane
Land" (perhaps Chihuahua, where these birds abound),
whence they had emigrated in the latter half of the
twelfth century. Regarding their history previous to
their entry into Anahuac we are ignorant. Legends
concerning it are plentiful enough, but all are obviously unworthy of credence, and must be dismissed
from consideration in a sketch of Nahua history,
which professes to deal with verifiable facts only. In
the study of Nahua history it is well to obtain a

mastery of facts at the outset, and to peruse subsequently all traditional matter, or the facts will be
in danger of submersion under the superincumbent
mass of legend. The very origin of the Aztecâ is un-
certain, but it is highly probable that they were of
Nahua stock. The catalogue of their wanderings
after reaching Anahuac is quite as untrustworthy as
that of their peregrinations before entering it, ·and
it will be advisable to commence their history here
with their appearance in Tecpanec territory. Suffice
it to say that they claimed to have sojourned at
Tzumpanco, Ehecatepec, and Tepayacac, and to have
been reduced to slavery by the chiefs of Culhuacan,
whence they journeyed to Chapoltepec, finally quit-
ting it to rid themselves of the exactions of the
Xaltocanecs. Upon their settlement near the Tecpanec pueblos, tribute was imposed upon them by
the chiefs of the confederacy, and soon what had been
mere marsh villages arose into the busy pueblos of
Tenochtitlan (Mexico) and Tlatelolco, situated on
the islands of the lake. Their chiefs were taken from
the Tecpanec pueblos, to whom they speedily became
invaluable allies.

With the assistance of the Aztecâ, the conquests
of the Tecpanec confederacy greatly increased,
Xochimilco, Mizquic, Cuitlahuac, and other pueblos
being subdued in rapid succession. Whilst the Tecpanecs were thus extending their territory the

Aculhuaque in the north were faced with an insurrection of the Otomi pueblos. It has been stated that Texcuco appealed for aid to the Tecpanecs, but there is no evidence in support of this. The Tecpanecs, however, invaded the Otomi territories, which they speedily overran, conquering the valley of Quauhtitlan, Xaltocan, and the mountain districts to the north-west.

The Aculhuaque had founded pueblos on the fringe of Texcuco, and of these Acolman and Cohuatlichan were desirous of freeing themselves from the yoke of the Chichimecs. Their policy was to ally themselves with the now powerful Tecpanecs under the aegis of the pueblo of Azcapozalco. Techotlalatzin, the chief of that pueblo, died in 1406, an event seemingly most provident for the chiefs of the community. Ixtlilxochitl, his successor, proved a weakling ; and the majority of these pueblos, hitherto in alliance with Texcuco, transferred their allegiance to the Tecpanecs. Upon this the chief of Azcapozalco demanded tribute of Ixtlilxochitl—to wit, raw cotton—a demand which was refused, if not on the first, then on a subsequent occasion. A three years' war followed the refusal, in which the Chichimecs seriously menaced the Tecpanecs suzerainty in the valley. But the Tecpanecs rallied, and with the assistance of Tenochtitlan (Mexico) and Tlatelolco, attacked Texcuco, drove Ixtlilxochitl from his possessions, and pursued him into the mountains where he was slain by the stratagem of a traitor. In reward for the part which they had taken in this campaign, the Mexicans received Texcuco as an addition to their territories, and Tlatelolco was placed in possession of Huexotla, while the chiefs of Acolman and Cohuatlichan were forced to pay homage to the Tecpanec rulers.

The second group of three pueblos now came into existence, being formed by Azcapozalco, Acolman, and Cohuatlichan, as the first triad had been by Xaltocan, Tenayucan, and Culhuacan. But, failing the support of Tenochtitlan and Tlatelolco, it was impossible for Azcapozalco to stand. This assistance was withheld, for the people of these pueblos found themselves too strong, and their markets too well patronised, to require the further assistance of the city under whose aegis they had grown into considerable communities. They refused the usual tribute to Azcapozalco, contenting themselves with a merely nominal gift of cereals and other foodstuffs, and requested permission to construct an aqueduct from the shore for the ostensible purpose of assuring themselves a suitable water supply. The Tecpanecs indignantly refused this request, alleging their suspicions of invasion which the proposed aqueduct would assuredly have facilitated, and at once took steps to ensure the future integrity of their pueblos by the ruin and reduction of Tenochtitlan and Tlatelolco, by strictly prohibiting all intercourse with their inhabitants, and placing an embargo upon all goods emanating from the rebellious pueblos. The chief of Tlatelolco was assassinated, and the chief of Tenochtitlan was captured, but took his own life ere summary vengeance could be executed upon him. His successor, Izcohuatl, assisted by thirteen chiefs, who were ever afterwards regarded as heroes by the Mexicans, fought a great battle with the Tecpanecs, defeating them with great slaughter, and captured Azcapozalco, in or about the year 1428. By this victory Tenochtitlan acquired the supremacy of the entire valley, and laid the foundation of her extensive dominion. From this event we may date the unquestionable predominance of Tenochtitlan or Mexico. Her subsequent alliance with Texcuco and Tlacopan formed the third triad of the lake pueblos. The former was placed under the rule of its rightful prince, Nezahualcoyotl, who, during the period of Azcapozalcan supremacy, had been a fugitive outcast. The tribute formerly paid to the Tecpanecs was diverted to the allied pueblos, between whom a perfect understanding existed.

A renascence of architectural and engineering activity followed upon the defeat of Azcapozalco. The people of Tenochtitlan constructed great causeways connecting the city with the mainland, so that in

time the south-western portion of the Lake of Texcuco
presented the appearance of a harbour fenced by
breakwaters. Such pueblos as resisted this policy at
the time were reduced to subjection, and the city of
Mexico became, through the erection of these works,
a fortress of almost impregnable strength. Her
conquests began to spread far beyond the Valley of
Anahuac. With the assistance of Texcuco and
Tlacopan, the Valley of Quauhtitlan, the northerly
Otomi districts, and the cotton district of Quauhnahuac, were overrun, and divided among the
allies. Motecuhzoma I (1436–1464) subdued much
territory south of Quauhnahuac, and indeed extended
the Mexican dominions almost to the limits they
had attained at the period of the Spanish Conquest.
This was also a period of great commercial expansion.
The Mexican merchant was frequently followed by
the Mexican warrior, and interference with Mexican
trade was made the pretext for further conquest and
appropriation of territory. From the cotton districts
the Mexicans procured tribute of the raw material,
which they utilised in the manufacture of clothing
and armour, whilst gold and precious stones formed
the contribution of the Mixtecs and Zapotecs. The
markets of Mexico became the nucleus of commerce
for the whole tract between Yucatan and the northern
boundaries of the present Republic. Conquest was
also achieved in the direction of the Mexican Gulf,

and Cuitlachtlan, Mixantlan, and Papantlan, were
rendered subject to the rule of Motecuhzoma I.

At the death of Motecuhzoma I, Axayacatl succeeded to the throne, reigning from 1464 to 1477, when
he was followed by his brother Tizocic (1477–1486).
Another brother, Ahuizotl, wielded the kingly power
from 1486 to 1502.   The chronicles of these reigns
announce the completion of the Mexican conquest of
the valley, and the virtual suzerainty of Tenochtitlan
over all the other neighbouring communities.

Motecuhzoma (Montezuma) II, virtually the last
of the Mexican kings, reigned from 1502 until the
coming of the Spaniards in 1520.   Originally a priest,
he was elected monarch, and proved himself a
courageous warrior and an able administrator.   The
coming of the Spaniards appears to have paralysed
his ability to think or act for himself, the widespread
superstition that the white men were the servants of
the sun-god Quetzalcoatl, who had once held sway
in Mexico, and whose return had been prophesied,
seemingly having preyed upon his mind.   The history
of his reign is the first chapter in the history of the
Spanish Conquest of Mexico, and, as such, has no
place in this work.

Fig. 1.   Mexico in the time of the Motecuhzomas.

(From the *Letters of Cortes*, Nuremberg, 1524.)

CHAPTER VI

I. MYTHOLOGY AND RELIGION

Mythology and Religion of the Nahua People—Evolution of the
Gods—Tezcatlipoca—Huitzilopochtli—Tlaloc—Quetzalcoatl.

THE religion of the Nahua was represented by
a polytheism comparable in its general aspects to
that of Greece, Rome, or Egypt, but differing from
them in various essential characteristics, such as the
prevalence of human sacrifice and ceremonial cannibalism with all their gruesome but picturesque rites.
More than one original influence is recognisable in
Nahuan mythology, as will be seen when we come to
examine the nature of the various deities who went
to make up its pantheon.

Many unfounded assertions have been made
regarding the belief of the Nahua in a universal
All-Father, a "god behind the gods." It is probable
that shortly before the Spanish Conquest of Mexico
there was a general movement on the part of the
cultured classes towards a belief in monotheism. But
concerning that movement our data are too imperfect
to permit us to speak with any degree of certainty.
As with the deities of Egypt, their especial priests were
wont to address the gods of Mexico in magniloquent
terms, as "endless," "omnipotent," "invisible," "the
Maker and Moulder of All," and "the one God

complete in perfection and unity." But it must be understood that these phrases were not applied to any particular god, but were merely terms of lauda- tion employed by the devotees of every individual deity to do him honour, and to exalt him above the other members of the pantheon.

When a people emerges from the hunter state and begins to place reliance upon agricultural labour as a partial or entire means of subsistence, it inevitably creates in its own imagination a class of divine beings whom it regards as essential to the growth and fertility of the crops or produce it raises, or the live stock it breeds. It is possible that concurrently with the evolution of these beings, the process of evolving other gods from still older forms, probably of an animistic or totemic origin (that is, nature and tribal spirits) may still proceed, as an examination of the genesis of the various Nahua deities will prove. But, except in rare instances, these latter usually become almost overshadowed by the elemental and fructifying deities which speedily arise upon the adoption of a settled mode of existence. With these deities of the soil man imagined himself in covenant. Inasmuch as he supplied the gods with food (human sacrifices) he was in turn provided with grain and the fruits of the earth. He averted the old age of the gods by assuring their rejuvenescence through the blood of sacrificed victims, and in return looked to them for assistance and sustenance. The *raison d'être* of the old totemic or tribal deities existed no longer, man not now being dependent upon their good offices for support and protection. These remarks of course allude to an advanced stage of agricultural development such as we have to deal with among the Nahua. Totemic influences still lingered in districts where they had developed marked local significance, but obviously not to such an extent as prevailed, for example, in Yucatan or Guatemala. There a perfect maze of local animistic or nature beliefs renders the elucidation of the characters, and even the identification, of the great national deities almost impossible, because of the manner in which the idiosyncrasies of local gods have been grafted upon one or other of the members of the higher pantheon.

A disquisition upon the evolution from minor spirits of deities presenting well-marked attributes is unnecessary here. The subject has been treated at length and with much erudition by many able writers, whose theories will be adapted to the elucidation of the characteristics of the various Nahua deities when they come under consideration.

Probably the most satisfactory mode of dealing with Mexican mythology will be found in the separate examination of the origin and attributes of the principal deities. We shall endeavour to depict the Mexican deities in the light of known facts,

while not hesitating to apply to the elucidation of
their origins and attributes such scientific methods
as may best illustrate the position they hold in
comparative mythology, that science of religion which
embraces the faiths of the world, great and small.

The Jupiter of the Nahuan pantheon, the god
par excellence, was Tezcatlipoca. His name signifies
"Fiery Mirror," from a shield of polished metal
which he was universally depicted as carrying. The
"civilisation" of this god, who was an Aztec deity,
would appear to have been effected only upon the
coming of that race to Anahuac, and their adoption of
its culture, as his attributes exhibit marks of having
been evolved by a people in a low state of mental
and social development. So far as can be ascertained
he was the personification of the Breath of Life. One
of his names, and that which probably gives the key
to his origin, is "Yoalli-Ehecatl," or "Night-Wind."
Now in the mind of savage man the wind is usually
the giver of breath, the great storehouse of respiration,
the source of immediate life. In many mythologies the
name of the principal deity is synonymous with that
for wind, and in others the words "soul" and "breath"
have a common origin. It has been suggested that the
Hebrew Jahveh (the archaic form of Jehovah) is
connected with the Arabic *hawah*, to blow or breathe,
and that Jahveh was originally a wind- or tempest-
god (Marti, *Geschichte*, § 17). Our word *spiritual*

is derived from the Latin *spirare*, to blow; the Latin *animus*, spirit, is the same word as the Greek *anemos*, wind, and *psukhe* has a similar origin. All are directly evolved from verbal roots expressing the motion of the wind or the breath. The Hebrew word *ruah* is equivalent to both "wind" and "spirit," as is the Egyptian *Kneph*. If we turn to the American mythologies, *nija* in the language of the Dakota means "breath," or "life"; in Netela *piuts* is life, breath and soul; the Yakuna language of Oregon has *wkrisha*, wind, *wkrishmit*, life. The Creeks applied to their supreme deity the name Esaugetuh Emissee, Master of Breath[1] and the original name for God in Choctaw was Hustoli, the Storm Wind. The Kiché *Hurakan*, a name borrowed from the tongue of Haiti, has given us our word *hurricane*. "In the identity of wind with breath, of breath with life, of life with soul, of soul with God, lies the far deeper and far truer reason," says Brinton, "of the prominence given to wind-gods in many mythologies[2]."

But although Tezcatlipoca was the Giver of Life, he was also regarded as a deity with power to take it away. In fact at times he appeared as an inexorable death-dealer, and in this guise he was named Nezahualpilli ("the hungry chief") and Yaotzin ("the

[1] See my art. on Cherokee Religion in Vol. III. *Encyclopaedia of Religion and Ethics*.

[2] *Myths of the New World*, p. 69.

Enemy "). But he was also known as Telpochtli
("the Youthful Warrior"), from the fact that his
reserve of strength, his vital force, never grew less,
and was boisterously apparent, as in the tempest.
He was depicted as holding in his right hand a dart
placed in an *atlatl* or spear-thrower, and in his left
his brilliant mirror-like shield and four spare darts.
As the wind at night rushes through the roads with
more seeming violence than it does by day, so was
Tezcatlipoca pictured in the Aztec consciousness as
rioting along the highways in search of slaughter.
Indeed seats or benches of stone, shaped like those
used by the chiefs of the Mexican towns, were placed
at intervals on the roads for his use, and here he
was supposed to lurk, concealed by the green boughs
which surrounded them, in wait for his victims.
Should anyone grapple with and overcome him, he
might crave whatsoever boon he desired, with the
surety of its being granted.

Tezcatlipoca was supposed by the Texcucans to
be the tutelary deity of Huitznahuac, one of the
quarters of their city. He was said to have guided
their fathers from the north to the Valley of Mexico.
But his worship appears to have been widely diffused
among all the Nahua peoples. He also seems to have
been regarded as a god of fate and fortune, and in these
varying attributes of his we seem to trace the possibility of his having been originally a fusion of several

local deities into one. But that he was primarily a god of wind and life-giving breath there is no good reason to doubt. His other aspects as a deity of fate and a death-dealer appear to have been after-thoughts.

The worship of Tezcatlipoca previous to the Conquest had so advanced, and so powerful had his cult become, that it would appear as if the movement would ultimately have led to a monotheism or worship of one god equivalent to that of the cult of Jahveh, the God of the Old Testament among the ancient Hebrews. To his priestly caste is credited the invention of many of the usages of civilised life, and it succeeded in making his worship universal. The Nahua people regarded the other gods as objects of special devotion, but the worship of Tezcatlipoca was general.

The festival of the Teotleco, or "coming of the Gods," well illustrates the paramount position occupied by Tezcatlipoca in the Aztec pantheon. In October the gods were supposed to return from their annual travelling, Tezcatlipoca being invariably the first to return. A heap of maize flour was placed at the entrance of his teocalli (temple-pyramid), and when footprints or other marks appeared upon it, his arrival was announced. Thus the security of the whole community was supposed to be assured.

The Toxcatl festival, held in May for the purpose

of inducing Tezcatlipoca and Huitzilopochtli the war-god to assist in procuring rain for the crops, was celebrated in a great sacred enclosure where copal incense was constantly burned to Tezcatlipoca. During ten days a priest of the god dressed in his symbolic robes, sounded his sacred flute or whistle (typifying the whistling of the wind) to each point of the compass. During this period the wicked went about in fearful awe, as upon the renewal of his covenant with mankind it was quite possible that Tezcatlipoca might turn and rend them. Thus we see that the conception of sin had arisen in the Aztec mind in connection with Tezcatlipoca, and to this we will afterwards refer more fully.

On the night previous to the festival, new garments were placed on the image of Tezcatlipoca, which was publicly exhibited. In the morning he was carried down the teocalli in a litter, and placed upon the ground. Young men and maidens attached to the teopan, or temple, then came forward with a thick rope consisting of strings of parched maize, or izquitl, which they placed round the image and its litter in the shape of wreaths. These withered wreaths, called toxcatl, symbolised the barrenness of the season, and from them the festival got its name. The entire purpose of the feast was to pray for rain. The image of Tezcatlipoca was escorted round the teopan, whilst the people scourged themselves. A war-captive was then sacrificed to Tezcatlipoca in the following circumstances.

Tezcatlipoca had a living representative selected from the war-captives of each year. He must be without spot or blemish, and upon selection at once assumed the garb and attributes of the deity himself. He took his rest during the day, and at night sallied forth, armed with the dart and shield of the god, to scour the highways. To his arms and legs small bells were attached, and he also carried the symbolical whistle of the deity. He was efficiently guarded, and until daybreak he walked the streets of the town, resting on the stone seats already mentioned. At a later date he was provided with companions in the shape of four beautiful maidens of high birth, with whom he passed his time in idle dalliance, and entertainments of every kind. He was fêted at the tables of the nobility as Tezcatlipoca in the flesh, and his whole existence was one prolonged round of pleasure. At length the fatal day of his doom arrived—that of the Toxcatl festival. He bade farewell to the partners of his joys, and set out for the teocalli, upon the steep side of which he broke his whistle and the other instruments which had conduced to the pleasures of his captivity. Arrived at the summit he was made one with the god whom he represented—that is, he was sacrificed in the usual manner, by having his heart torn out.

Tezcatlipoca appears to have been one of the few Mexican gods in any way related to the expiation of sin. The Mexicans symbolised sin by excrement and in the Borgian Codex[1] Tezcatlipoca is represented as a turkey-cock (Chalchiuhtotolin = emerald fowl), to which ordure is offered. He is thus the sin-eater, as was Tlaclquani, the earth-goddess.

Huitzilopochtli was the Aztec god of war, the Mexican Mars. His origin is wrapped in an obscurity which has proved too difficult of elucidation for many savants. Tylor calls him "an inextricable parthenogenetic compound deity." That he is not so inextricable as would at first sight appear we will endeavour to make plain ; but first it will be well to relate briefly the myth dealing with his supposed birth, and to examine what the older writers on Mexican mythology have to say concerning him, ere we attempt to dissipate the very substantial clouds which shroud his origin.

It is related that his mother Coatlicue or Coatlantona ("Female Serpent," or "Serpent-Robe"), a devout widow, was one day in the temple of the sun-god, when she was surprised by a ball of brilliantly coloured feathers falling at her feet. She picked it up, and placed it in her bosom, and was shortly afterwards

[1] For other representations of this phase of Tezcatlipoca see the Borgian Codex, p. 27; Vaticanus B, p. 6: or Borgian, p. 4 and Vat. B.

aware of pregnancy. Her family, enraged at what they considered her disgrace, were about to slay her, when Huitzilopochtli was born, brandishing his spear, and calling upon his mother to be of good heart, for he would slay those who had offended her. This he speedily accomplished, and after many warlike adventures ascended to heaven, where he obtained a place for his mother as the Goddess of Flowers.

The name Huitzilopochtli signifies "Humming-bird to the Left," and from this it has been surmised that he was originally a totem of the colibri bird, common in Mexico. This theory was strengthened by the fact that his left leg was adorned with the feathers of the humming-bird.

Among the North American tribes, snake-charming is regarded as the highest test of proficiency in magic, and the serpent is the symbol of lightning, the divine type of warlike might. Now magic brings victory in war. A fragment of a serpent was regarded as the most powerful and efficient "war-physic" it was possible to obtain. To signify his invincibility in war the Iroquois represent their mythical king Atalarho clothed completely in black snakes, so that when he wished for a new garment he drove away those he wore and called upon others to take their places. So with Huitzilopochtli; his mother is Coatlicue, the Robe of Serpents. Huitzilopochtli's idol was surrounded by serpents, and rested upon

serpent-shaped supporters. His sceptre was a single
snake, and his great drum was of serpent skin. With
the serpent in American mythology is usually associated the bird.   Thus the name of the god
Quetzalcoatl is translated "Feathered Serpent," and
instances could be multiplied of cases where the
separate conception of the bird and serpent had been
unified. Huitzilopochtli is undoubtedly one of these ;
hence his humming-birds' feathers. To sum up, we
may regard him as a deity arising from the twin
primary ideas of the serpent which typified the
lightning, the symbol of warlike might (the dart or
spear of the divine warrior), and the humming-bird,
which was regarded as a harbinger of summer, that
period when the snake- or lightning-god had power
over crops.

Huitzilopochtli was represented as wearing on his
head a plume of humming-birds' feathers, while his
face and limbs were barred with stripes of blue. He
carried in his right hand four spears and in his left
a shield on whose surface were five tufts of down
arranged in form of a quincunx. The shield was
made of reeds with eagles' down placed upon it,
and was known as teueuelli. His spears were also
tipped with tufts of down instead of flint, and were
known as tlauaçomalli. These were the weapons which
were placed in the hands of those destined to a sacrificial death by combat, because, to a certain extent,

Huitzilopochtli represented the conception of a warrior's death on the temalacatl, or stone of sacrifice, on which the Aztecs placed the strongest of their enemies to do battle with their own picked warriors.

Huitzilopochtli was the war-god of the Aztecâ, and, in the form of a humming-bird, was supposed to have led them to the site of Mexico from their original home in the north. In fact one of the districts of the pueblo of Anahuac, that of Mexico, from which the entire city later took its name, was called after a title of his, Mexitli.

But Huitzilopochtli had another significance besides that of a war-god pure and simple. As the serpent-god of lightning he was associated with the summer and its abundance of crops and fruit. The Algonquians believed that the rattlesnake, the lightning-serpent, could grant prosperous breezes or raise ruinous storms. They made it the symbol of life. In the same way the Aztecâ believed that Huitzilopochtli could grant them suitable weather for their crops, and they actually placed an image of the rain-god Tlaloc upon the summit of the mound which supported the teocalli of Huitzilopochtli, so that the war-god might be enabled to observe his actions and compel him, if necessary, to exert his rain-making powers, or to abstain from sending floods.

The principal festival of Huitzilopochtli was the

Toxcatl, held immediately after that of Tezcatlipoca, and similar to it. Another feast with a like significance was held in May, and one in December, at which an image of the god was modelled in dough, kneaded with the blood of sacrificed children, and pierced by the presiding priest with an arrow. This was to signify that the influence of Huitzilopochtli was dead for the rest of the year. Another festival in his honour was the Panquetzaliztli, the "raising of the flag," the signal to begin annual warfare against the Tlascaltecs, the people of Tlascala, for the provision of sacrificial victims. In battle, the Huitziton or Paynalton, a small image of Huitzilopochtli, was carried by the priests in front of the troops to incite them to deeds of prowess.

The high priest of Huitzilopochtli, Mexicatl Teohuatzin, was the Pontifex Maximus or High Priest of Mexico. In fact all the priests of Huitzilopochtli held office by right of descent. This chief exacted implicit obedience from all castes of the priesthood, and was regarded as being next to the monarch in power and dignity.

Tlaloc was the god of rain, both in its fructifying significance and in its aspect of disastrous floods. In Mexico the success of every crop depended entirely upon the rainfall, and Tlaloc, who was supposed to dwell in the mountains which surrounded Anahuac,

took an important place in the national pantheon.
His likeness was more generally sculptured than that
of any of the other Mexican deities, and he is usually
represented in a semi-recumbent position, with the
upper part of the body raised upon the elbows, and
the knees half drawn up, probably to represent the

Fig. 2.   Statue of the god Tlaloc found at Chichen-Itza.

mountainous character of the country whence came
the rain.   He was accompanied by a goddess, Chalchihuitlicue, his wife, who bore him a numerous progeny,
the Tlalocs (the Clouds).   He sometimes held in his
hand a serpent of gold to represent lightning, for
water-gods are closely identified with thunder, which

dwells in the hills and accompanies heavy rains.
Indeed Tlaloc manifested himself in three ways;
the flash, the thunderbolt and the thunder (Gama,
Descrip. de los dos Piedras, II. p. 76). He was
appealed to as inhabiting each of the cardinal points,
and every mountain-top, but his image faced the east,
whence he was supposed to come. His robe was
crossed by ribbons of silver typifying mountain
torrents, and decorated with feathers of yellow, green,
red, and blue, symbolic of the four cardinal points.
Before his image was usually placed a vase containing
every description of grain. To the Mexicans his
dwelling, Tlalocan, was the plenteous and fruitful
paradise, where all worthy persons went after death.
Those who were drowned, struck by lightning, or who
had died of dropsy, were regarded as the chosen of
Tlaloc. Those of the common people who did not
die such deaths went to the Land of Mictlan, Lord
of Death.

In the native manuscripts the face of Tlaloc is
usually represented as of a dark colour, with a large
round eye, a row of long tusks, and over the lips an
angular blue stripe curved downwards and rolled up
at the ends. These characteristics are supposed to
have been produced originally by the coils of two
snakes, their mouths with long fangs in the upper
jaw, meeting in the middle of the upper lip.

Tlaloc had several important festivals. Ramirez

states that the Toltecs immolated several maidens
every year in his honour (*Notas y Esclarecimientos*),
and the Aztecâ sacrificed hundreds of children to him
annually. If they wept it was regarded as a happy
omen for a rainy season. His chief festival was the
Etzalqualiztli ("when they eat bean food"), held on
May 13, on which date the rainy season usually
commenced. The feast lasted about a month. The
Mexican year commenced with another festival in
his honour, the Quauitleua, held on February 2.
At the Etzalqualiztli the priests of Tlaloc plunged
into a lake, imitating the sounds and motions of
frogs, which, as representing water, were under
his special protection. Indeed Chalchihuitlicue, his
wife, is often represented by a small figure of a
frog, cut out of a whitish-green stone, a material
invariably used for the statues of Tlaloc.

Artificial ponds sacred to Tlaloc were constructed
in the mountains, and there human beings were
sacrificed to him. Near them large burying-grounds
were situated, and offerings to the god were also
interred in their vicinity. Torquemada (*Monarchia
Indiana*) relates that his statue was placed on the
mountain of Texcuco, and Ixtlilxochitl mentions that
five or six young children were yearly sacrificed to
him, their hearts being torn out, and their bodies
buried. The mountains of Popocatepetl and Teo-
cuinani were regarded as his special preserves,

according to Torquemada[1], and on the slope of the latter was situated his ayauchcalli (house of prayer) in which stood his idol, carved out of the green stone chalchihuitl.

The Mexicans believed that the production of food brought about a condition of senility in the gods, especially in the case of the maize and water gods. This they attempted to combat by giving them a season of rest. This was done by holding every eight years a festival called the atamalqualiztli, or "feast of porridge balls and water," in which everyone returned for the nonce to the conditions of savage life. The most picturesque part of the festival consisted of a dance round the teocalli of Tlaloc, in costumes representing beasts, birds, and insects, whose various sounds were mimicked by the dancers. The object of this performance was the amusement of Tlaloc, who was supposed to be exhausted by the production of the fertilising rains. A lake was filled with frogs and water-snakes, and the people entered this, catching the reptiles in their mouths and devouring them while yet alive. No grain food was permitted to be eaten except a water-porridge of maize.

Quetzalcoatl was a deity of the Nahuan-speaking pre-Aztecan people of Anahuac. He was regarded

[1] Tom. ii. lib. vi. cap. 23.

as a god alien in some measure to the Aztec people, and had only a limited following in Mexico, the city of Huitzilopochtli. His principal sanctuary was in

Fig. 3.   The god Quetzalcoatl.

Cholula, and from thence along the route which the Toltecs are said to have traversed, traces of his worship are found until we reach Cozcatlan, a centre of the Pipils in the present republic of San Salvador.

We will first examine the myth of Quetzalcoatl,
and then attempt to unravel his somewhat perplexing
personality. We shall later have to consider him
according to various authorities as Air-god, Sun-god,
and "Culture-hero."

Quetzalcoatl was regarded as "the father of
the Toltecs," and according to one migration-legend
of the advance of the Toltecs from north to south,
he was the seventh and youngest son of the
Toltec Abraham, Iztacmixcohuatl. His name signifies
"Feathered Serpent," or "Feathered Staff."   He
became ruler of Tollan, and by his mild sway and
the introduction of the arts and sciences, did much
to further Toltec advancement, of which indeed he
may be said, in the terms of myth, to have laid the
foundations.   However the time came when he was
persecuted by the cunning wizards, Tezcatlipoca
and Nauhollin, the former of whom, descending
from the sky as a spider, by means of a fine web,
gave him pulque (liquor distilled from the maguey
plant) to drink. Becoming intoxicated he forgot
his chastity, and he was doomed to exile from
Anahuac. He buried his treasure of gold and silver,
burned his palaces, and changed the cocoa trees into
mezquites and dispatched the birds from Tollan to
the district of Mexico. Alarmed at the state of
matters brought about by his departure, the wizards
besought him to return, but he declined on the

ground that the sun required him. He proceeded to Tabasco (the fabled land of Tlapallan), and embarking upon a raft of serpents, floated away. The Annals of Chimalpahin and of Quahtititlan[1] state that he cast himself upon a funeral pyre and was consumed, and that his ashes flew upwards and were metamorphosed into brilliantly coloured birds. His heart, also ascending, became the morning star. The Mexicans said that Quetzalcoatl died when the star became visible, and they called him "Lord of Dawn." They believed that when he died he became invisible for four days, and that he wandered for eight days in the underworld, after which the morning star appeared, when he was supposed to have ascended his throne as a god.

An examination will now be made of the theories of those who see in Quetzalcoatl a god of the air alone. Their contention is that he is connected with the cardinal points, and wears the insignia of the cross which symbolises them. "He has a protruding trumpet-like mouth, for the wind-god blows....His figure suggests whirls and circles. Hence his temples were built in circular form....The head of the wind-god stands for the second day of the twenty day-signs of the Mexicans, which was called Ehecatl, 'wind.'"[2] The same authority, however, credits Quetzalcoatl

---

[1] *Anales de Mus. Nac. de Mex.* Vol. III.
[2] Eduard Seler, *Mexican Picture Writings*.

with a dual nature in his Essay on "Mexican Chronology," where he states that "The union of fire and
wind which presents itself in the Zapotec name of
the Mexican image of the second day-sign is also
probably the best explanation of the dual nature
which seems to belong to the wind-god Quetzalcoatl,
who now appears simply as a wind-god, and again
seems to show the true characteristics of the old god
of fire and light."

For a still more probable elucidation of the
nature of Quetzalcoatl we must examine the theory
which makes him the ruler of the sun, who had left
his abode for a season for the purpose of instructing
mankind in the arts of life, and who is ultimately
displaced by the gods of a later period, described
as cunning enchanters. The fact that Quetzalcoatl
was represented as a traveller with staff in hand signifies his solar character, as does the fact that under his
rule the crops flourished mightily and spontaneously.
Indeed he represented the agency by which the earth
was made to bring forth fruit. Gold and precious
metals were also found in profusion during his reign,
and gold is a metal invariably connected with the
sun by barbarous peoples. Other conclusive con-
nections may be found in the fact that in the
pinturas the solar disk and semi-disk are almost
invariably shown in combination with the feathered
serpent as symbolic attributes of Quetzalcoatl. The

solar disk is also frequently found in connection with small images of Quetzalcoatl, sometimes attached to the head-dress, whilst in other specimens he appears to be emerging from the luminary.

Quetzalcoatl possessed alleged variants in several parts of Mexico and Central America, notably Gucumatz in Guatemala and Kukulkan in Yucatan, both of which names signify "feathered serpent." Kukulkan is undoubtedly identical with Dr Paul Schellhas's "God B"[1]. Like Quetzalcoatl he is often represented in the pinturas as paddling in a canoe. In the Dresden Codex he is depicted as planting maize-seeds, as on a journey, and as possessing the body of a serpent. In figure he is pictured as the possessor of a long proboscis-like nose, with a tongue or teeth hanging out. Fewkes, Förstemann, Düsseldorf, and Professor Cyrus Thomas have all seen in Kukulkan a "serpent-and-rain" god. If this be so, it is only in so far as he is also a solar god—the serpent with tail in mouth being a symbol of the solar disk. The cult of the feathered snake in Yucatan was most certainly a branch of sun-worship. In tropical latitudes the sun draws the clouds around him at noon. The rain falls from these clouds to the accompaniment of lightning and thunder—symbols of the heavenly serpent. Therefore the manifestation of the heavenly serpent bore a direct solar significance, and no statement that

[1] *Deities in the Mayan MSS*, p. 16.

Kukulkan is a mere serpent-and-water deity—the serpent being associated with water because of its sinuous movement—presents any satisfactory elucidation of the characteristics of this god.

There are not wanting evidences of the northern origin of Quetzalcoatl, which if they are well founded would go to prove that his more southern aspects as Quetzalcoatl, Kukulkan, and Gucumatz, had been evolved in consonance with the climatic conditions of regions into which he was later adopted. Recent researches amongst the Indians of British Columbia, whence the Nahua in all probability came, prove that a mythology exists among them, the central figure in which is obviously closely akin to Quetzalcoatl. This deity is worshipped as the Man of the Sun, and quite apart from the sun himself, as was Quetzalcoatl in Mexico. The Quaquiutl say that the sun descended as a bird, and assumed a human shape before settling among them. Kanikilak is his son, who carries the arts of civilisation all over the world[1]. Quetzalcoatl descended first of all in the form of a bird, which was ensnared by the Toltec hero Hueymactzin who accidentally caught it in a fowler's net.

That Quetzalcoatl was indeed a wind-god as well as a god of the sun and the heavens as was Jupiter,

[1] *Brit. Assoc. 5th Report on the North Western Tribes of Canada*, 1889, pp. 29–51; F. Boas, *Bull. Am. Geo. Soc.* 1896, No. 3.

will be seen from his various titles. Some of these
were : Ehecatl, the air ; Yolcuat, the rattlesnake ;
Tohil, the rumbler ; Huemac, the strong hand ;
Nanihehecatle, lord of the four winds ; Tlaviz-calpan-
tecutli, lord of the light of the dawn. The whole
heavenly vault was his, as were all its phenomena.
If this sovereignty overlaps that of Tezcatlipoca, it
must be borne in mind that the latter was the god
of a later age, and of a fresh body of Nahuan immigrants, and as such a decided rival of Quetzalcoatl,
who probably was similarly opposed to Itzamna, a
Mayan deity of Yucatan.

The priesthood of Quetzalcoatl were a body
separate from the priests of the other gods, his
worship being to some extent antipathetic to that
of the other deities of Anahuac.

CHAPTER VII

II. MYTHOLOGY AND RELIGION

The Mythology and Religion of the Nahua People continued—
The Food Gods—The Earth Goddess—The God of Sacrifice—
The Fire God—The Moon-Goddess—the Sun-God—Parent
Deities—God of Death—God of the Chase—Drink-Gods—The
Planet Venus.

THE deities who presided over the food-supply
and agriculture of Anahuac formed a regular group,

each of whom personified the maize plant in one of
its varied aspects. Of these Xilonen represented the
xilote or ear of the green corn. But the goddess of
maize proper was Chicomecohuatl (Seven-serpents).
She had received this name in allusion to the fertilising
properties of water, which was typified by serpents.
The spring feast (April 5) of this goddess was called
Hueytozoztli, or the Great Watch, a festival which
was accompanied by a general fast and the decoration
of dwellings by bulrushes, which had been sprinkled
with blood drawn from the extremities of the devotees
of the Corn-mother. The statues of the gods which
they kept in their houses were also enwreathed, says
Torquemada, and it is probable that he alludes to the
Tepitoton or small tutelary or household deities of
the lares and penates type which the Nahua kept in
their dwellings, and which forcibly remind us of the
Ushabtiu figurines of the Egyptians which they
buried with their dead. The worshippers then proceeded to the maize-fields, where they cut the tender
stalks of the maize, and bedecked them with flowers,
afterwards placing them in the calpulli or common
house of the village. They then went before the
altar of Chicomecohuatl and engaged in mock combat
before her shrine. The maidens of the community
carried bundles of maize from the harvest of the
previous year, which they presented to the goddess,
afterwards returning them to the storehouses so that

they might be used as seed for the coming year. Torquemada especially states that Chicomecohuatl was averse to the shedding of human blood, but that in all probability human sacrifices formed part of the ceremony, "as it was the universal practice to make them in all their festivals."

Among the Tepitoton the Maize Goddess was invariably represented, and before each of the diminutive figures the worshippers placed a basket of food, on the top of which was a cooked frog, having on its back a piece of a cornstalk stuffed with pounded maize and vegetables. This frog was symbolical of Chalchihuitlicue, the wife of Tlaloc the rain-god, who, it was supposed, must co-operate with Chicomecohuatl to ensure a plenteous harvest. A frog was also sacrificed in order that its vitality might pass into the soil.

The midsummer festival of Chicomecohuatl called Hueytecuilhuitl, lasted eight days, commencing when the plant had attained its full growth. At this festival the women of the community wore their hair unbound, and in the ceremonial dances which formed the chief part of the sacrifice, they shook and tossed it as a symbolical hint to the maize-plant to grow correspondingly long. Quantities of chian pinolli (infusion of chian seed) were drunk and maize porridge was partaken of. The teopan or temple was illuminated, and wild dances were performed within

its precincts. A female captive or slave with face
painted red and yellow to represent the colours of
the maize-plant, had previously undergone a long
course of training in the dancing school, and now
exhibited her powers in a spirited manner. This
was the Xalaquia who, all unaware of the horrible
fate which awaited her, danced gaily in the hope of
conjugal union with the god, which she had been led
to suppose would be her lot. Night after night she
danced, and on the last day of the rites she was
accompanied in her exercises by the women of the
pueblo, who at the same time recited the deeds of
the goddess. The dance lasted until daybreak, when
the chiefs of the community made their appearance,
and danced the death dance, in which the doomed
girl also took part. A procession was then formed
to the place of sacrifice on the summit of the teocalli.
When it was reached the victim was stripped of her
gay attire, and the priest, brandishing his knife of
iztli, made an incision in the breast, tore out the still
palpitating heart, and offered it to Chicomecohuatl.
The vitality of the victim was supposed to enter the
soil and afford fresh life and sap to the venerable
goddess, exhausted with the labours of the past season.
Hence the name "Xalaquia," which signifies "She who
is clothed with the sand," and until the death of the
sacrifice it was unlawful to eat of the new corn.

The appearance of Chicomecohuatl, to judge from

her idol which rests in the National Museum at Mexico, was hideous in the extreme. It is girdled with snakes, and on the underside the symbolic frog is carved. For generations this idol was identified with a fictitious mythical character, which the absurd scholarship of the eighteenth and nineteenth centuries designated Teoyaominqui. The first to point out the error was Payne[1] who showed that this figure reproduces the primitive fetish which it superseded. The original figure of the goddess was extemporised in the maize-field out of bundles of maize, with pieces of paper pasted thereon to represent her features, and these characteristics are reproduced in the image in question.

The presence of a male corn-god side by side with a female deity of the same type, has caused much difficulty to arise in the minds of many students of Mexican mythology. The fact is that Aztec theology stipulated for an earth-mother, Teteoinnan (mother of the gods), or Tocitzin (our grandmother), of whom Centeotl, the male maize-spirit, was the son. Older belief, perhaps Toltec, had embalmed the idea of one female maize-spirit named Chicomecohuatl. Centeotl was the name of a corn-god, who was the offspring of the earth-mother of later Aztec theology, and this earth-mother must be regarded as distinct from Chicomecohuatl. The victim sacrificed at the

---

[1] *Hist. of the New World called America*, Vol I. p. 424.

midsummer festival of that goddess employed her last days in weaving aloe fibre into a ritual dress for the maize-god. Robed in this it was thought that he temporarily represented the earth-goddess, so that he might receive her sacrifice. The blood of victims was offered to the god in a vessel decorated with feathers. When he tasted this he uttered such a groan that it is recorded that such Spaniards as were present grew terror-stricken. All present then took part in the niticapoloa, or "tasting of soil," which consisted in raising a little earth on one finger to the mouth and eating it.

Centeotl the son must not be confounded with Centeotl the mother, who is in reality the earth-mother, Teteoinnan. Each was separately worshipped in different teopans, but the two were closely allied. After the death of a female victim sacrificed to Centeotl, her skin was taken to the temple of Centeotl the son, and worn there in the succeeding ritual by the officiating priest.

Three other earth-goddesses were worshipped in Mexico, but these possessed a purely local significance. One was the earth-mother of the Zapotecs. The other was the goddess of a people much nearer Mexico, Cihuacoatl (Woman-serpent) or Tonantzin (Our Mother), the earth-mother of Xochimilco. The name "serpent" probably designated her connection with the earth, as in the case of Chicomecohuatl.

Her worship was one of the most sanguinary in the Mexican Valley, flesh-food being her staple diet. In fact once a week the insatiable cravings of this deity for human flesh were met by the sacrifice of a human victim. Another great earth-goddess of the Mexican Valley was the Tonantzin of Tepeyacac, whose teopan was rased to make a foundation for the Church of Our Lady of Guadaloupe.

The Progenitrix or Mother of the Gods, Toci or Teteoinnan, was an earth-goddess of venerable antiquity. She was the goddess of purity, of purification, and of the eradication of sin. Her symbol was the domestic broom, and she had a festival, the Ochpanitzli, "broom-feast," or "house-cleaning festival," that implement symbolising cleanliness. Cotton as a material for female employment was one of the chief attributes of Toci, and her headband or turban is represented as being made of that article. A strip of raw cotton hangs from her ear-pegs, and loose cotton is bound to the end of a spindle which she wears between the hair and the headband[1].

Tlaelquani (dirt-eater), or Tlazolteotl (god of ordure), designated the dirt-eater, was an earth-goddess. She was the eradicator of sins, to whose priests the people went to confess their sins in order

---

[1] E. Seler, *Mex. Pict. Writings of Alex. Humboldt*, Fragment i.

to be freed from them. She is represented as eating ordure, the hieroglyphical symbol for sin, which proves that sin had a very real significance in the Nahuan mind. The necessity for confession in Mexico was confined to offences against the sacredness of marriage.

Xipe ("the Flayed") whose original home was near Yopi, a valley on the Pacific slope, but whose worship was widely spread throughout the highlands, and in Mexico, is usually represented as being clothed in a flayed human skin. At his festivals victims not only had their hearts torn out in the usual manner, but their corpses were afterwards flayed, and the skins were worn by the devotees of the god during the twenty days following the festival. This feast was called Tlacaxipeualiztli, or "man-flaying." Another name of Xipe was Tlatlauhqui Tycatl. He is usually depicted as of a red colour. Mexican monarchs and leaders of armies in later times assumed the dress of Xipe—the crown made of feathers of the roseate spoonbill, the gilt timbrel, the jacket of spoonbill feathers, and an apron of green feathers, lapping over like tiles. In the Cozcatzin Codex we see a picture of King Axayacatl dressed as Xipe in a feather skirt, and having a tiger-skin scabbard to his sword.

Xipe's shield is the tlauhteuilacachiuhqui—a round target covered with the rose-coloured feathers of the spoonbill, with concentric circles of darker tint on the surface. Sometimes it is divided into an upper and a lower part, the former displaying an emerald on a blue field, and the latter a tiger-skin design. The god was regarded as three forms: as the red god, having the colour of the roseate spoonbill; as the blue god, having the colour of the blue cotinga; and as a tiger, the three shapes probably corresponding to the three regions, heaven, earth, and hell, or the three elements, fire, earth, and water.

Xipe is seldom represented in the manuscripts in any other form than that of the Red God. He is of course the god of human sacrifice, which he personified, and in some ways may be regarded as originally a Yopi equivalent of Tezcatlipoca.

Nanahuatl or Nauauatzin (Poor leper) is a deity of a peculiar type. It was supposed that persons afflicted with certain diseases, syphilis, or leprosy, had been set apart by the moon for his service. Indeed in Nahua the words for leprous, eczematous, or syphilitic also mean "divine." The myth of Nanahuatl well illustrates this belief. Before the sun was created, humanity dwelt in gloom. A human sacrifice alone could hasten his appearance. Then Metztli, the moon, led forth Nanahuatl, and the victim cast himself upon a funeral pyre in which he was consumed. Metztli followed him, and as she disappeared the sun rose above the horizon. The myth is of course a reference to the consuming of the spotted or starry night in the flame of the dawn.

Xolotl is a god of southern origin, possibly Zapotec, and may represent fire rushing down from the heavens, or light flaming upwards. In the manuscripts the setting sun devoured by the earth is placed in opposition to him. In the Mexican legends he appears as the representative of human sacrifice; and is probably identical with Nanahuatl. He also appears to be closely akin to Xipe. He was regarded as the twin brother of Quetzalcoatl.

The Fire-God was designated Tata (Our Father), Huehueteotl (Oldest of Gods), and Xiuhtecutli (Lord of the Year). He was typified by the representation of a man painted in the colours of fire, with a head-dress of green feathers, a black face, and a yellow-coloured serpent placed upon his back to symbolise the serpentine nature of fire. Like Tezcatlipoca he possessed a mirror of gold to denote his connection with the sun, from which all heat emanated, and to which all heat was subject. The first duty of an Aztec family on rising in the morning was to consecrate to Xiuhtecutli a piece of bread and a libation of drink. He was thus analogous to Vulcan, who, besides being the creator of thunderbolts and conflagrations, was also a divinity of the domestic hearth. Once a year the fire in every Mexican house was extinguished, and rekindled by friction before the idol of Xiuhtecutli. The Nahuan infant passed through a baptism of fire on the fourth day of its life, up to which time a fire lighted at its birth was kept alive in order to nourish its existence (Sahagun, *Hist. N. E.*, lib. VI. cap. 4).

The Moon-Goddess, also called Yohuatlicitl (Lady of Night), and Tecziztecatl (Cause of Generation), had also a darker phase, as goddess of night, cold, and dampness, the bringer of miasmatic fogs and rheums, of ghosts, and of the causeless sounds of night. Her name in this capacity was Metztli. Metztli sends evil dreams and desires upon man. She was connected with water like the moon-goddesses of all mythologies; and all maladies, as in the case of the Egyptian goddess Isis, were regarded as the effects of her anger. "We are all of us under the power of evil and sin because we are children of water" says the Nahuan formula of baptism. Women stood in special relation to the moon, as in Greece, Rome, and Egypt.

The principal goddesses, other than the earth- and corn-goddesses already dealt with, were Xochiquetzal and Zapotenantli.

Xochiquetzal, the Nahuan goddess of love and

sexual pleasure was also designated Itzcuinan, or "Bitch-Mother," to express her great fecundity. She is in reality only a variant of Tonantzin, the old earth-goddess, in the guise of a beautiful fecund female who typifies the fertility of the soil. Zapotenantli, mother of the Zapotecs, was a goddess borrowed from that people by the Mexicans, and was practically identical with the earth-goddess of Mexico.

Sun-Worship was extremely popular throughout Mexico. The sun was regarded as the *teotl*, the god *par excellence*. The name of the sun, Ipalnemohuani, "He by whom men live," shows that the Mexicans regarded him as the source of all life, and the heart, the symbol of life, was usually offered up in sacrifice to him, the vital organ being plucked from the bodies of animals used for food and held up to the rising luminary. Even the hearts of victims sacrificed to Huitzilopochtli and Tezcatlipoca were offered up to the sun, as if restoring to him the life which he had given. Blood was the favourite offering to the sun, and in the pinturas he is depicted as licking up the gore of the victims of sacrifice with his long, tongue-like rays. The sun must eat if he was to be sustained, and terrible was the ritual which provided for his subsistence (see Codex Borgia).

A cardinal belief of the Mexicans was that eternity had been broken up into cycles, the various epochs in which were marked by the destruction of successive suns. In the period preceding that under review the sun, it was supposed, as well as the entire universe, had been destroyed by a great deluge, and some such catastrophe was anxiously looked for at the conclusion of each "sheaf" of fifty-two years. The old suns were dead, and the present sun was no more immortal than they. At the end of one of the "sheaves" he would not reappear. He must then be sustained through daily sacrifices; hence the ceaseless hostilities with other tribes to procure material for these sacrifices.

The sun was therefore the god of warriors, as he would give them victory in battle, in order that they might supply him with food. The rites of this warrior-worship were held in the Quauhquauhtinchan, or "House of the Eagles," an armoury provided for a regiment of that name. On March 17 and December 1 and 2, according to Duran (*Hist. de las Indias*, cap. 88), at the ceremonies known as Nauhollin or "Four Motions," alluding to the trembling appearance of the sun's rays, they gathered in the armoury for the purpose of despatching a victim or messenger to their lord the sun. The victim, a war-captive, was placed at the foot of a stairway consisting of sixty steps leading up to the Quauhxicalli, or "Cup of the Eagles,"—the stone of sacrifice. Above this was an enormous golden representation of the sun on a great wheel of fire. The victim, clothed in red

striped with white, wearing white plumes in his hair,
and carrying a staff decorated with feathers and a
shield covered with tufts of cotton, bore on his
shoulders a bundle of eagles' feathers and paint to
enable the sun, to whom he was the emissary, to
decorate his face. He was then requested to greet
the sun, and to ask him to look favourably upon his
sons below, to present him with the staff for the
purpose of helping him on his journey, the shield
for his defence, and the feathers and paint for his
adornment. This the victim promised to perform,
when he was despatched upon his journey.

The Mexican warriors believed that after death
they would dwell in the Home of the Sun, serving
him continually, intoxicated with heavenly delights,
and partaking in the cannibal feasts offered to him
on earth.

The victim, however, was granted a chance for his
life. He was led to the temalacatl or fighting-stone,
and if he could succeed in defeating six Mexican
warriors he was permitted to return to his people.

The principal festival of the sun was held in
spring at the period of the vernal equinox, before
the idol of a deity known as Totec, or "our great
chief." Totec was a solar deity, but as his worship
had been adopted from the people of a neighbouring
state, he was only regarded as a minor god, although
typifying the sun-god. His festival appears to have

consisted in a symbolical slaughter of all the gods for the purpose of vivifying the sun, each of the gods being symbolically slain in the person of a victim. Totec was attired in the same manner as the victim despatched twice a year to assure the sun of the fealty of the Mexican warriors. The victim was forced to undergo the gladiatorial form of combat previously described as being held on the temalacatl, and upon receiving a wound was immediately sacrificed. But the festival was a seasonal rather than a military one, for bunches of dried maize were offered to Totec.

The Nahua recognised two deities as the original father and mother of all human beings, much in the same way as the Greeks regarded Kronos and Gaia. Their names were Ometecutli and Omeciuatl, which mean Lords of Duality or of the two sexes. They were also designated Tonacatecutli and Tonacaciuatl, Lord and Lady of our Flesh or of subsistence. They were in fact regarded as the sexual essence of the creative deity, or of deity in general. They were given the first place in the calendar to denote that they had existed from the beginning, and are usually represented as clothed in rich colours. The male is sometimes identified with the sky, the sun, or the fire-god, who is at the same time the god of the chase and of war, the female deity being identified with the earth or the water.

Mictlan was the Aztec god of death, or rather of that Hades to which the dead repaired. He was indeed in all respects identical with the Greek Hades or Pluto. He is generally represented as a monster whose capacious maw is ever open to engulf the spirits of the dead. Although his dwelling-place Tlalxicco was called the navel of the earth, it is often located in the far north. With the peoples of Central America, as with other races, the north was regarded as a place of desolation, famine, and death. Like the Greek Hades, no punishment awaited the dead in Mictlan, the entire atmosphere of the place merely presenting a dreary and dark appearance, where those souls who had died deaths unfitting them for the paradise of Tlalocan, were doomed to spend a shadowy and meaningless existence. This deity had a counter-part in Mayan mythology in the god Hun-Hau or Ahpuch, who is designated as Yum Cimil, Lord of Death, in the popular superstition of the Yucatecs of the present day. He was surrounded by a species of demons called Tzitzimimes.

Mixcoatl was the Aztec god of the chase, and had been adopted from the Otomies. The name signifies "Cloud-serpent," and is stated by Brinton to represent the tropical whirlwind. On p. 35 of the same work (*Myths of the New World*), he states that Mixcoatl, whose name by the way he now spells differently, was the God of Hunting, and is of course correct in the latter surmise. There are many such gods in all mythologies. The hunter-god is usually identified with thunder-clouds, because of the fact that the lightning is supposed to represent arrows, and he is generally depicted with animal characteristics. A well-known instance of this will occur to nearly everyone who is familiar with the legend of Herne the Hunter with his deer's head and antlers. Mixcoatl is only the cloud-serpent inasmuch as he is a wielder of the lightning as a weapon of the chase. Nearly all American tribes have similar deities. He is represented with a bundle of arrows in his hand to typify the thunderbolts. It is of course possible that Mixcoatl was originally an air- and thunder-god older than either Tezcatlipoca or Quetzalcoatl, and that when he was displaced from his lofty position by one of these deities, a niche had to be found for him somewhere in the pantheon, so that he took his place as a god of hunting. Dr Seler describes him as being very nearly related to the morning star, and it will be recalled that various Grecian hunter-deities had close relations with the same luminary.

Patecatl was one of the Mexican gods of pulque. When a man was under the influence of this liquor, the Mexicans, like other barbarous peoples, believed that he was under the influence of a god or spirit. But there were other drink-deities, and the commonest form under which the drink-god was worshipped was the rabbit (Ome-tochtli = two-rabbit), this animal being considered as being utterly devoid of sense. The greater the degree of debauchery to which the worshipper desired to descend, the greater the number of rabbits he worshipped, and as the greatest number of rabbits commonly calculated by the Mexicans was four hundred, the Centzontotochtin-teopan signified the temple of four hundred rabbits, where the last degree of drunkenness was permitted.

Tequechmecauiani was a drink-god to whom it was necessary to sacrifice, if one wished to avoid suicide by hanging during intoxication, and Teatlahuiani was worshipped if death by drowning was apprehended ; but if a mere headache was feared, then Quatlapanqui, "The Head-splitter," must be placated, or else Papaztac, "The Nerveless." There were Ome-tochtli for each particular trade, sacrifice to whom was supposed to avert the after-consequences of indulgence in pulque, but there was only one Ome-tochtli for the upper class, Cohuatzincatl, a name signifying " He who has grandparents."

Many of these gods had names which connected them with various localities, for example, Tepoxticatl, the god of Tepoxtlan.   On the whole it is safe to infer that they were originally deities of husbandry who imparted virtue to the soil, as pulque imparted strength to the warrior[1].

Of the planets the only one worshipped by the Mexicans was Venus, which was regarded by them as a god. They called it Citlalpol, "the great star," and Tlauizcalpantecutli, "lord of the dawn." When it rose in the morning they stopped up the chimneys of their houses, so that no harm of any kind might enter with its light. In the court of the great temple at Mexico there stood a column called Ilhuicatitlan, which signifies "in the sky," or "towards heaven." On this pillar a figure representing the planet was painted, and prisoners were sacrificed before it when the planet Venus reappeared in the sky (Sahagun, Vol. II. App.). The planet has some connection with Quetzalcoatl (q.v.). In the Tonalamatl or calendar Tlauizcaltantecutli is represented as lord of the ninth division of thirteen days, beginning with Ce coatl, which means "one serpent." In the Codex Telleriano-Remensis and Vaticanus A, he is depicted as having a white body with red longitudinal stripes and with a deep black painting about the eyes like a domino mask, bordered by small white circles. His lips were painted red. The red stripes on a white ground are merely inserted to accentuate the fact of his

[1] See Seler, *Temple Pyramid of Tepoxtlan*, Globus v. 73, N. 8.

whiteness. This white colour is probably intended to symbolise the hazy half-light which emanates from the planet, while the black paint on the face is symbolic of the night sky. As the star of evening he is sometimes represented with the face of a skull to signify his descent into the underworld whither he follows the sun. The periods of his revolutions were carefully and accurately observed by the Mexicans and Mayans, as can be seen by reference to the Borgian and Vaticanus B codices in Lord Kingsborough's work.

CHAPTER VIII

III. MYTHOLOGY AND RELIGION

Cosmogony—Priesthood—Temples—Ritual—Sacrifice and Cannibalism.

THE Nahua believed that eternity was broken up into a number of æons, each of which was determined by the period of duration of a separate sun. They supposed the destruction of the existing state of things to be impending at the end of each "sheaf" of fifty-two years, and imagined that the sun would fail to appear on the morrow following the last day of the fifty-second year. In this manner had terminated the previous æons, which must in no way be confounded with the "sheaves," these being merely arbitrary chronological fragments of these æons. Each successive æon had its own particular sun. The various authorities on Mexican antiquities are not in agreement as to the number of ages in the Nahua mythology, but the preponderance of testimony appears to be in favour of four antecedent æons, each of which ended in disaster because of flood, tempest or famine. The period of time from the first creation to the commencement of the present æon may have been either 15,228, 2316, or 1404 solar years, the discrepancy arising because of the equivocal meaning of the numeral signs expressing the period in the manuscripts. There is no more agreement as regards the sequence of these æons than there is regarding their number. The Codex Vaticanus gives it as water, wind, fire, and famine ; Gama has hunger, wind, fire, and water ; Humboldt, hunger, fire, wind, and water ; and Boturini, water, famine, wind, and fire. Ternaux-Compans embraced the theory that the four suns possess a mystical correspondence to the domination in turn exercised over the globe by its four principal elements, but it does not appear that Nahua philosophy was aware of such a doctrine. Humboldt suggested that the suns connected with these four epochs were "fictions of mythological astronomy modified by obscure reminiscences of some great revolution" (*Vues des Cordillères*, Vol. II. p. 118).

The probability is that the adoption of four ages arose from the sacred nature of that number, which is illustrated, for example, in the four cardinal points. Again four was the number of secular days in the Mexican week. In all likelihood this theory of the ages of the world had existed in various forms among the Nahua before it received that in which we now have it, and as this latter form was accomplished long after the final arrangement of the calendar, it was almost possible that the myth shaped itself upon the tonalamatl. In fact it is stated by Eche-varria that a number of suns or æons was agreed upon at a congress of astrologists within traditional times (*Hist. de la Nueva España*, lib. I. cap. 4). As will be pointed out in the chapter on the calendar, these signs occur in the sequence earth, air, water, fire, in correspondence with the days marked with the symbols Calli, house; Tochtli, rabbit; Acatl, reed; Tecpatl, flint. This sequence, commencing with Tochtli, rabbit, is given as that of the suns in the Codex Chimalpopoca. The present period of the world began, as the Mexicans believed, in the year 1 Tochtli, when the heavens, which had fallen on the conclusion of the previous æon, were again raised up.

The several priesthoods of the Mexican gods were all under the rule of a " Pontifex Maximus," the

Mexicatl Teohuatzin, or High Priest of Huitzilo-pochtli, which office was hereditary. The priesthood of Tezcatlipoca was a special cult, and by far the most enterprising of all. The High Priest of Quet-zalcoatl bore the name of the deity he served, and was second in importance to the Mexicatl Teohuatzin; but the worship of Quetzalcoatl in Mexico was quite subordinate to that of the lower conceptions, whereas in Cholula it was the religion *par excellence.*

The priestly caste embodied all the science and wisdom of the country. Education was under their control, and was so directed that the student remained under the priestly domination to the end of his days. That the priestly order was very numerous is shown by the fact that no less than five thousand persons officiated in the great temple of Mexico, their rank and functions being apportioned with the minutest detail. The Mexicatl Teohuatzin, or "Mexican Lord of Divine Matters," wielded considerable political influence, and was a member of the royal council. The priestly caste was essentially aristocratic in its basis.

The places of worship of the gods were called teopan, and were generally constructed in the form of a square or oblong court surrounded by walls, in the centre of which arose a teocalli or sacrificial pyramid, consisting of several platforms, access to

which was given by a winding pathway encircling
the whole structure. Occasionally, however, flights
of steps directly ascended each side of the teocalli.
On the summit was placed a small temple, in which
the idol of the presiding deity was kept. Within the
walls of the teopan were situated the houses of the
officiating priests. The teocalli is of course an
evolutionary form of the original "high place" or
mount of sacrifice, and not, as in the case of the
Egyptian pyramid, a form evolved from the primitive
cairn. The description of the great teopan of Mexico
in the chapter on architecture will give an idea of
these edifices.

The ritual of the several priesthoods was elaborate,
and has been described more or less in dealing with
the various festivals of the gods, but several points
remain to be considered. The Spanish Conquistadores
were surprised to discover that the religion of the
Aztecs coincided, in many of its outward aspects,
with their own Catholicism. The rite of baptism,
for example, symbolised the washing away of natural
sin, and the eating of the dough image of Huitzilopochtli kneaded with blood, upon the occasion of his
second festival, was an act emblematic of consubstantiation, as was indeed the devouring of the
bodies of sacrificial victims, who were supposed by
the act of sacrifice to have become one with the god

to whom they were immolated. Confession was also noticed by the Conquistadores, but with the Nahua it was not a customary rite. It was usually made late in life, when the ability to sin further was probably past, and the rite might not be repeated. But it is not clear whether absolution was granted to the penitent or not. However in the nature of things it is unlikely that confession would have been made unless absolution followed. As already mentioned, confession was confined to sins of the flesh.

The act of sacrifice has been mentioned on several occasions in connection with the various festivals. When the victim reached the summit of the teocalli, he was seized by five priests who laid him on a stone of sacrifice. Four of them secured his hands and feet, while the fifth depressed his head. The sacrificial stone was convex in shape in order to raise the breast of the victim, so that the officiating priest might easily operate thereon. The chief priest then advanced holding a knife of iztli, or obsidian, with which he made a deep gash in the breast of the victim. He then inserted his hand in the wound and wrenched out the still palpitating heart, which he first held up to the sun and then cast into a basin of copal. This vessel was placed in such a position that the rich steam of blood and incense ascended to titillate the nostrils of the god.

After the sacrifices had been consummated, the remains of the victims were usually given to the warriors who had captured them, who, with their friends, banquetted upon them. But we must not altogether regard these disgusting repasts as the revels of flesh-famished savages. We have remarked that at the root of the idea of Nahuan cannibalism was the doctrine of consubstantiation, or oneness with the god to whom the victim was sacrificed. We find this desire for unity with deity, and in fact with superior humanity, running through the whole of savage and barbaric life. Many peoples, among others the South Sea Islanders, devour the remains of their relatives, in order that they may partake of their good qualities.

CHAPTER IX

THE CALENDAR SYSTEM OF THE NAHUA

THE importance of the Calendar System in the study of Nahua life and mythology cannot well be overestimated. By its aid the entire civil and religious machinery of Nahuan existence was regulated, and its mythological significance was paramount.

It was a simple cycle of 365 days perpetually repeated without any intercalation or correction.

The lack of intercalary days resulted in process of time in its receding relatively to the seasons, and

Fig. 4. The Aztec Calendar Stone.

all alleged amendments and intercalations must be regarded as fictitious.   The works of the older Spanish authors give no indication of the presence

of any intercalations or corrections, and Torquemada
expressly denies that they ever existed. "They knew
nothing of the six hours by which the year exceeds
365 days," he says; "hence their year had no fixity,
and did not begin punctually as our year does."

For the proper comprehension of the Mexican
Calendar System it is necessary to understand that
in one Nexiuhilpilitztli (sheaf of fifty-two years),
there were really two separate cycles—one of 52
years of 365 days each, and another of 73 groups of
260 days each. The first represented the Mexican
idea of the solar year, and consisted of eighteen
periods of twenty days each, or so-called months,
with five days added, these last being known as the
nemontemi, or "bad" or "useless" days, which will
be treated of later. These must not be confounded
with intercalations. The cycle of 73 groups of
260 days, each counted as 20 times 13, was the
birth-cycle.

The date of the commencement of the Mexican
year according to European chronology, has been
hotly disputed by various authorities. Two obvious
reasons will at once occur to persons acquainted
with the history of ancient Mexico and the habits of
barbarous peoples, to account for the discrepancies in
the various theories of the commencement of the
Mexican year, viz. :

(1) The foundation of the various Mexican

communities at different dates, and the consequent variation between their chronologies, owing to the length of time during which some had been in existence prior to others.

(2) The custom of rulers and ecclesiastics in shifting the incidence of festivals, through the gradual discrepancy between the Mexican year and the real solar year, of which practice there is good evidence.

The cempohualli, or twenty-day period, was the fundamental basis in the reckoning of time. These periods were wrongly termed "months" by the Spanish writers. Each day was denoted by a sign such as "wind," "house," "smoke," etc. This reckoning ran perpetually without reference to the year, and formed the practical calendar of the people, each of whom was called after the sign of the day of his birth. All commercial matters were regulated by this reckoning, which was divided into four periods of five days each, in which interval markets were held in the principal towns. These shorter periods were designated by the sign of their middle or third day, and when the "year of the sun," consisting of four ordinary years, was represented in the calendar, each of these years was also indicated by the sign of the middle day in the five-day periods, and each sequence received the series of names Calli (house), Tochtli (rabbit), Acatl (reed), and Tecpatl (flint).

The calendric year of the Nahua was a multiple

of the twenty-day cycle, and consisted of eighteen
cempohualli, and on this reckoning the system of
feasts and sacrifices was founded. The religious year
proper consisted of only 360 days, the remaining five
days or nemontemi being regarded as ominous and
unwholesome. During these nemontemi no work was
performed, excepting what was absolutely necessary,
as it was popularly believed that what was done on
those days would have to be compulsorily undertaken
during the ensuing year. For civil purposes, however,
the signs of the day-cycle ran continuously (without
regard to the end of each year of 365 days) throughout
the "year of the sun," or for four years, so that the
sign cipactli recovered its place in every fourth year
as the initial day of the year. For the reckoning of
festivals, on the other hand, the cycle remained on
its original footing of eighteen periods of twenty days
each, the first of which began on the first day of the
year, no matter what sign denominated that day in
the civil calendar. The twenty-day periods of the
ecclesiastical calendar thus corresponded only once in
every four years with those of the secular almanac.
They were obviously regarded as periods of time,
each of which had its appropriate festival.

We have seen that the years themselves were
incorporated into groups. Thirteen years constituted
a Xiumalpilli or bundle, and four of these bundles a
Nexihuilpilitztli or "complete binding of the years,

or thirteen years of the sun." Each ordinary year had thus a double aspect, first as an entire entity, and secondly as a fractional part of the "year of the sun"; and for the purpose of designating the years in this latter aspect, they were represented by signs taken from the four fractional parts of the cempohualli of twenty days, Tochtli, Acatl, Tecpatl, and Calli. Thus every year had a double notation, a number showing its place in the series of the tlalpilli or bundles from 1 to 13, and a sign-name showing its place in the "year of the sun." Thus each year in the series of fifty-two in the "Bundle of Years" had a different designation.

The twenty-day period, reckoned on a different principle, was also brought into requisition as a birth-cycle of 260 days, so that in the "completed bundle of years" of 52 solar years, there were 73 of these birth-cycles. This cycle had originally been a lunar one of thirteen days, marked by the names of thirteen moons, and although the entire series of signs used in the calendar was employed in it, it remained lunar in its character. The change consisted in counting the numerals from 1 to 13 in a parallel series with the twenty names of days used in the civil reckoning, the sign in the civil series corresponding to the number 1 forming the thirteen-day group commenced by it. A series of twenty periods of thirteen days each was thus evolved by the application of these numeral signs to the twenty-day period.

Thus no two days throughout the year were designated alike. For example, the sign cipactli took *ce* or 1 in the first period of thirteen days and *chicuei* or 8 in the second, *yei* or 3 in the third, and so on. Some of the signs were regarded as of good omen, and others as of evil import.

CHAPTER X

THE LIFE OF THE NAHUA

Government—Military System—Agriculture—Metals—Art—
Commerce—Domestic Life—Dress—Dwellings.

THE form of government in vogue among the Mexicans at the time of the Spanish Conquest was that of an elective monarchy, the electoral functions being vested in a committee of four of the principal nobles (Telpopochtin) appointed by their own body, who, on the death of the reigning prince, selected his successor from among the brothers, or failing them, the nephews of the deceased sovereign, thus restricting the succession to one family.

The sovereign was assisted in the conduct of state business by councils who met in various halls in the royal palace. The chief of these councils, which probably included the four electors, dealt with the government of the provinces, the collection and disposal of revenue, and the more important matters of general interest.

The Telpopochtin or nobility exercised the judicial, military, and ecclesiastical functions, holding all the highest positions of trust.

The legislative power was vested in the monarch, but the possibility of a despotic government was minimised by the establishment of a judiciary, appointed by the crown, and consisting of supreme judges over each of the great cities and their dependent territories, who held office for life, and exercised civil and criminal jurisdiction, from which there was no appeal even to the throne itself. An inferior court of three members sat in each province for the trial of civil and criminal causes, an appeal to the supreme judges being available in the latter. Popularly elected magistrates were distributed throughout the country for the settlement of petty causes, and a still more subordinate class of officers, similarly appointed, exercised supervision over a certain number of families, and reported all infractions of the law to the higher authorities.

The controlling power in the Mexican army was exercised by the sovereign, assisted by a council or staff, the chief officer being called Tlacochcalcatl, or Keeper of the House of Darts, the other members

being the Tezcacoacatl, keeper of a second arsenal;
the Atempanecatl, governor of the prison where
victims were confined; Tillancalqui, superintendent
of the military college; and several minor officers.
The great object of war being the capture of sacrificial
victims, a kind of knightly order was formed, the
members of which held rank and wore uniforms
according to the number of captives they had secured.
Every telpochtli, or nobleman, on entering the army
had to act as attendant to some warrior, and earn
his promotion by his valour and skill, preferment
through favouritism being unknown.   On his marriage
he attained the rank of warrior or tequihua, and gave
a farewell feast and gifts to his fellows.

From a scientific point of view, the tactics of the
Mexican forces were not on a high plane, their method
of attack consisting in alternate charges and retreats,
the use of ambuscades and surprises, and the light
skirmishing incidental to guerilla warfare.

Agriculture in the Mexico of the Aztecs had
reached that stage in which the hunter condition has
given place to existence on a settled alimentary basis.
If the soil was not so carefully farmed as that of the
Maya country, the husbandry was at least as skilful
as it is in the average European agricultural district
of to-day. The peasantry were scattered over the
face of Anahuac, dwelling in small villages under
the shadow of a great pueblo. Of these communities

there must have been not less than five hundred, and
in most respects they closely resembled the village
communities of the Old World. A great central
house, calpulli, was the nucleus of the village and
formed a meeting-place for its freemen; but in later
times it was superseded by the *tecpan* or house of the
chiefs, around which the peasants' huts clustered.
The land laws were careful to distinguish between
those lands assigned to chiefs, cultivated by the serfs,
and those apportioned to the villagers for their own
use. Certain of the lands were merely the fiefs of
the teopans and provided these institutions with
material for clothing and general provisions. The
headman of the district possessed a manuscript map
of it on which the various lines of demarcation and
the several varieties of land were carefully marked out.
Agriculture was closely identified with the national
religion, as will have been seen in the chapter which
deals with that phase of Mexican life. Indeed from
its inner workings the marvellously intricate calendar
system had been evolved. But agriculture had also
its imperial aspect for this people. The bulk of the
public taxes was paid in the produce of the fields,
and all those individuals who were not engaged in
war, that is in the business of procuring victims for
the upkeep of the gods, must perforce busy themselves with agricultural pursuits. The work was
chiefly done by men, but the women assisted in

sowing the seed, and in the lighter labours of the
field. There appears to have been no lack of true
agricultural knowledge among the Nahua. They
took especial care not to permit the land to become
fallow or exhausted by over-use, and their system of
irrigation compensated for the natural dryness of the
soil. Heavy penalties overtook those who destroyed
standing timber or growing crops, and large granaries
were a feature of every Nahua community.

It has been advanced as an argument against the
general intelligence of the Nahua that they were
unacquainted with the use of iron, in which the soil
of their country was extremely rich. This of course
resulted from the fact that its preparation required
so many processes to render it fit for use that it
appeared to be a waste of labour to the Nahua, or
by the fact that its close incorporation with the soil
itself prevented its being noticed by them. They
were, however, acquainted with gold, silver, lead, tin,
and copper, and with an amalgam of the two latter
metals which, when used with a silicious dust, could cut
the hardest substances, even precious stones. When
we read of the huge "emeralds" fashioned by the
Aztecs into symbolical figures, it is necessary to
remember that these were in reality pieces of
chalchihuitl, a species of green jade. In the preparation of metals and their formation into artistic
and ornamental shapes, their artists were unsurpassed,

and the goldsmiths of Spain admitted their inferiority
to the Indian artificers.   Besides tools of metal, they
used *itztli*, or obsidian, which is found in abundance
in Mexico.   This *itztli* they made into razors and
knives, and placed serrated pieces of it in the edges
of their *maquahuitls* or wooden `swords.   They also
used it for the sacrificial knives with which the breasts
of victims were opened, previous to their hearts being
torn out.

Sculpture and pottery had reached a very high
stage of excellence among the Nahua.   Indeed, on
the whole, their art was on a level considerably
higher than that of the palmy days of Egypt.   It
was not burdened with the same conventionality
as was the Egyptian, and its representations were
much more natural in every respect.   The grotesque
certainly prevailed, but it was a grotesqueness which
bore within it the seeds of a higher artistic excellence.
The Aztec art was of course largely an offshoot
from the art of the older civilisations which had
flourished in Anahuac, and indeed in many instances
exhibited marked signs of deterioration.   The Nahua
were a nation of sculptors, and the foundations of
modern Mexico are said to be built upon the sculptured
relics of the past.   The sculpture of the Mexicans
consisted of bas-reliefs and ornamentations for the
bases and sides of the teocalli.   Very few examples
of it remain, but chief among them is the great

Fig. 5.   Terra-cotta masks and heads found at Teotihuacan.

calendar stone now in the Museum of Mexico, upon
which are depicted the signs of the Nahua cycle of
time. The Mexicans do not appear to have arrived
at that pitch of perfection in sculpture, of which
statuary, as apart from mere bas-relief, is capable of
achievement. So far as their pottery is concerned, it
was superior to anything manufactured by European
peoples at an epoch of similar development. Such
objects as have been recovered from the wreck of
the Spanish Conquest exhibit marked individuality
and high artistic ability. In the textile arts the
Aztecs were extremely skilful, and from the cotton
grown in the warmer regions of the country they
spun a fabric almost as fine as silk, which they
coloured with the most consummate art, cochineal
being the principal dye employed. In feather-work
they excelled, and the national genius appears to
have found its chief expression in this art. From
the gorgeous plumage of the humming-bird, parrot,
and other tropical birds, they wove the most wonderful
garments and tapestries. The brilliancy and nice
gradations of colour of these feather mosaics won
the rapturous applause of the artistically inclined of
Europe upon their introduction subsequent to the
Conquest.

The method of barter by which the business of
Mexico was carried on, was conducted in the market
places of the principal pueblos, which were opened

once a week for the purposes of commerce. The currency of the country consisted of feather quills stuffed with gold dust, and bags of cocoa. All the necessaries and luxuries of life were exhibited in the booths in these market places, and jewellers, fruiterers, tobacconists, pulque-sellers, poulterers and florists spread their wares to attract the public. The Spanish Conquistadores actually state that, on their first entry into Mexico, they beheld barbers' shops or booths in which men were being shaved with razors of obsidian.

The pursuit of trade was considered an honourable calling amongst the Mexicans, and, although there was no distinction of caste as in Egypt or India, it was usual for a son to follow his father's business. Each trade had its own district in the cities, its own chief, its own customs, its own deity, and so on. The mercantile community enjoyed special honour. With a richly-loaded and well-armed caravan the Aztec merchant travelled from place to place, dealing in slaves, stuffs, jewellery and other marketable commodities, and also bore with him costly presents from the sovereign to the chiefs whom he visited, receiving others in return, and licences to trade. If a hostile reception was accorded him, he might appeal to arms, employing the soldiers who accompanied him ; or the central government would very probably take his quarrel upon their own shoulders, using it as a pretext for extending the imperial sway.

The domestic life of the Aztecs exhibited a considerable degree of refinement. Their manners, while approaching oriental dignity, did not prevent the display of cordiality and affection. Polygamy was freely practised. The women enjoyed equal consideration with the men in respect to social ceremonies, attending at banquets, though not sitting at the same tables. The cleanly habit of ablution before and after meals was customary amongst them, while after dinner the men sat and smoked, some of them using snuff.

The table was well supplied, the viands including substantial meats, such as turkey, vegetables, and fruits, confectionery and pastry, with all kinds of delicate seasonings and sauces. Occasionally a revolting dish was added in the shape of human flesh, elaborately dressed, a slave being sacrificed in celebration of some religious festival. The dishes on the table were of gold and silver. The liquid refreshments included pulque and other light beverages. At the close of the repast the young people engaged in dancing, whilst their elders sat and sipped pulque and gossiped, occasionally getting intoxicated, a misdemeanour which was overlooked in old age, though severely punished in youth. Many of the Mexican nobility employed minstrels and jugglers to entertain their guests, the former singing ballads in honour of their lords and on other topics, whilst the latter performed feats of strength and legerdemain with considerable skill.

The costume of the upper classes consisted of a *tilmatli*, or cloak, thrown over the shoulders, made of various qualities of cotton, according to the rank of the wearer, and a *maxtlatl*, or loin cloth, of considerable length. These articles were often richly and elegantly embroidered, with deep fringes or tassels, and figures. In colder weather the *tilmatli* worn was of fur or feather-work. A favourite cloth, which was capable of taking a permanent dye, was woven of rabbit hair and the skin of other animals. The women wore several skirts or petticoats of various lengths, with ornamental borders, and sometimes also loose flowing robes reaching to the ankles, the quality of the materials depending upon the position of the wearer. No veils were worn, and the hair was allowed to hang loosely over the shoulders.

The higher officers wore magnificent and picturesque dresses. Their bodies were covered with a closely fitting vest of quilted cotton (*escaupil*), of such thickness as to be impenetrable to the light Indian missiles of warfare. In the case of the wealthier officers, this was occasionally replaced by a light corselet of thin gold or silver plates, over which was worn a feather-work surcoat. Their helmets were made of wood fashioned in the shape of an animal's head, or of silver surmounted by a

panache of feathers ornamented with jewels and
gold. Gorgeous gold, silver, and gem collars and
bracelets formed part of their attire. The ears,
underlips, and sometimes the nose, were occasionally
decorated with pendants of gems or gold crescents.

The garb of the common soldiers consisted merely
of the *maxtlatl*, or loin cloth, of coarse white stuff,
made from the thread of the aloe, called *nequen*.
Warriors ranked according to the number of captives
they had taken, those only having one prisoner to
their credit being plainly clothed, wearing no dis-
tinctive head-dress, and carrying a plain shield. The
dress became more ornate with each additional
capture, and when the number reached six, the
successful soldier attained the rank of Ocelot-Eagle,
wearing an ocelot skin, richly plumed, as a helmet.

The weapons of the Aztecs consisted of long
copper- or flint-tipped spears, slings, and darts, with
two or three points, attached to long cords, so that
they could be torn away again from the body of an
enemy. They also used bows and arrows. Those of
high rank carried a *maquahuitl*, or wooden sword,
furnished with a row of teeth made of flint.

The houses of the poorer classes were made of
reeds and mud. The nobility dwelt in large mansions,
seldom of more than one storey in height, built of
a red porous stone (*tetzontli*), quarried near the city.
The flat roofs (*azoteas*), were protected by stone

parapets, so that each house was a fortress. These
were generally covered with beds of flowers, or laid
out as gardens. The best apartments were hung
with gay cotton draperies, and the floors covered
with mats and rushes. The furnishings consisted of
low stools, made of single pieces of wood elaborately
carved, and mats, used as beds, thickly woven of
palm leaves, with cotton coverlets, and sometimes
canopies.

The structural form of the better-class dwellings
was that of a quadrangle with a court in the centre,
surrounded with porticoes embellished in porphyry
and jasper. The meaner dwellings were built of
unbaked bricks resting on a stone foundation, and
occasionally had wooden rafters in the roof.

CHAPTER XI

Antiquarian Remains—Architecture—Manuscripts.

BUT few architectural remains of the Nahua
survive. The best popular account of these is
furnished by Charnay in the first part of his *Ancient
Cities of the New World*. There are many excellent
handbooks upon the ruins of the Mayan civilisation,
but few have investigated the Mexican remains,
probably because of their scanty nature.

Fig. 6.   Teocalli of Xochicalco.

Fig. 7.   Teocalli at Papantla.

A description of the chief temple of Mexico as
given by one of the Spanish invaders may assist in
the formation of an adequate idea of the magnitude
and grandeur of such structures. This temple was
erected by Ahuizotl in honour of the god Huitzilopochtli, in the centre of the city within an enclosure
girt by walls 4800 feet in circumference. These were
constructed of rubble-stone laid in mortar, coated
with plaster, polished on both sides, and lavishly
sculptured, serpents figuring most frequently ; hence
they were designated Coetpantli, or walls of serpents.
On each side was a building, the lowest storey of
which gave access to the enclosure. The great
temple inside the court was a parallelogram in
form, measuring 375 feet by 300 feet, and was built
in six stories, each smaller than the other, in a
terrace-like formation. The walls were composed
of a mixture of rubble, clay and earth, covered with
large stone slabs carefully cemented and thickly
coated with gypsum. The upper platform, reached
by a flight of 340 steps which passed round each of
the terraces, was surmounted by two three-storied
towers, 56 feet high, the two upper stories being of
wood and only accessible by ladders.

In the lower storey of the teocalli were situated
the sanctuaries of the deities, their colossal statues
being concealed by magnificent draperies, and at
their feet stood the stone of sacrifice, made of green

jasper. The walls and floor were bespattered with human blood. In all the temples a sacred fire was kept perpetually burning, as it was supposed that its extinction would entail national disaster. In Mexico alone six hundred braziers were kept burning night and day. Forty smaller temples surrounded the principal one, amongst which was that of Tlaloc, reached by a flight of fifty steps ; that of Quetzalcoatl, which was circular and crowned by a dome, with a low door representing a serpent's mouth, through which worshippers had to pass ; and that of Ilhuizatlican, dedicated to the planet Venus, at the very moment of whose appearance above the horizon a victim had to be sacrificed. In one of the teocallis an immense cage was placed for the reception of foreign gods, so that they could not succour their worshippers. The bones of the victims were collected in the Quauhzicalco, the skulls being deposited in the Tzompantli, an immense oblong pyramid, in which the Spaniards alleged that they discovered 136,000 heads.

The court formed the largest portion of the enclosure, and within it immense crowds gathered to assist at the sacrifices, and in the gladiatorial combats. It was surrounded by the dwellings of thousands of priests, women, and children, charged with the care of the temples and their precincts, and was kept in a scrupulous condition of cleanliness.

Teotihuacan, twenty-five miles north of Mexico, has yielded much of interest to the explorer, the remains discovered by Charnay being the pyramid of the moon, the pyramid of the sun, the citadel, the palace, and " The Path of Death " or cemetery. The pyramid of the sun was the larger, being 680 feet at the base by 180 feet in height, divided into four stories ; but the intermediate gradations are almost effaced. The temple had a colossal statue of the sun made of a single block of stone, with a hollow breast containing a plate of fine gold. This statue was destroyed by Zumárraga, first bishop of Mexico, and the gold seized by the Spaniards. The interior of the pyramid was built of clay and volcanic pebbles, thickly layered with white stucco.

The citadel is a huge quadrilateral enclosure, measuring 1950 feet at the sides, surrounded by four embankments 19 feet high and 260 feet thick, surmounted by fifteen pyramids, while a fifth and narrower embankment towards the centre is occupied by a higher pyramid, and connects the north and south walls. Although called a citadel, the structure is shaped like a vast tennis-court, and was probably used not as a citadel, but for public ceremonials.

The palace of Teotihuacan presents similar features to that of Palpan. The rooms are, however, considerably larger, one having a side of 49 feet. The walls, built of stone and mortar and thickly cemented, slope for three feet and then rise perpendicularly, the total thickness being six feet seven inches. The roof was supported by pillars. The floors are coated with mortar, stucco, and cement, and ornamented with figures, with a border round the sides. Red, black, blue, yellow and white are still distinguishable.

The Path of Death, or cemetery, is composed of a series of small mounds, or *tlateles* (tombs), arranged symmetrically in avenues terminating at the sides of the great pyramids, and faced by cemented steps, which were probably used by the spectators of the funeral obsequies.

Manuscripts and Writing.

The Nahua possessed a system of writing which may best be described as pictographic, that is to say, that events were recorded by descriptive pictures. Most of these are written on paper made of agave, but some are painted on deerskin. The pictographic system in use by the scribes was applied to the purposes of daily life. The germs of a phonetic system may be observed in the treatment of names, which are generally represented by one or more objects, the names of which bear a resemblance to that of the subject depicted. For example that of the emperor Ixcoatl is represented by the figure of a serpent (coatl) pierced by obsidian knives (iztli), and the name of Montezuma or Motequauhzoma, by a mousetrap (montli), an eagle (quauhtli), a lancet (zo), and a hand (maitl). A syllable could be expressed by an object whose name commenced with it, so that the figures sometimes represent their full phonetic value, and sometimes only that of their initial sound. But the efforts of the artist were directed more to the idea than to the sound. However the scholarship of to-day can successfully elucidate in great measure the general drift of a Mexican manuscript, even if the more involved meanings it contains are incapable of interpretation.

As the result of Spanish intolerance but few of these manuscripts remain, thousands of them having been destroyed shortly after the Conquest. It must not be thought that every Mexican was capable of reading these codices. Their interpretation, which was a traditional one generally learnt by heart, and largely consisting of speeches attributed to the various figures represented, was in the hands of a class called *Amamatini* or *Amapoani*, " One who knows or reads the paper."

BIBLIOGRAPHY

Acosta, José de—Historia Natural y Moral de las Yndias. Seville, 1580.

Alzate y Ramirez—Descripcion de las Antiguedades de Xochicalco, 1791.

(A very inexact account of discoveries at Xochicalco.)

Bancroft, H. H.—Native Races of the Pacific States of America, 1875.

(Of considerable value as a compilation of nearly the whole field of literature relating to aboriginal America, which it presents almost without comment.)

Boturini, P. L.—Idea de una nueva historia general de la America Septentrional. Madrid, 1746.

(This collection is the fruit of eight years' research in the monasteries of Mexico, and contains a number of MSS important to the study of the history of the country.)

Charnay, Desiré—Ancient Cities of the New World (English translation). London, 1887.

(A clear and definite account of the architecture and antiquities of the archæological sites in Mexico and the ruined cities of Central America, but displaying little deep acquaintance with the subject.)

Clavigero, Abbé de—Storia Antica del Messico. Cesena, 1780. (English translation. London, 1787.)

Cortes, Hernando—Cartas y Relaciones al Emperador Carlos V. Paris, 1866.

8—2

De Bourbourg, Abbé Brasseur—Histoire des Nations Civilisées
  du Mexique et de l'Amérique Centrale. Paris, 1857–59.
  (A work which must be used with the utmost caution. The
knowledge of the Abbé concerning Mexico was most profound,
but his leanings towards the marvellous sadly discounted his
scholarship.)
Diaz, Bernal—Historia Verdadera de la Conquista de Nueva
  España. Paris, 1837.
  (Valuable as the testimony of an eye-witness of the Conquest
of Mexico.)
Gomara, F. L. de—Historia General de las Yndias. Madrid, 1749.
Humboldt, Alex. v.—Vues des Cordillères, et Monuments des
  Peuples Indigènes de l'Amérique. Paris, 1816. (Eng. trans.
  by Mrs Williams.)
Ixtlilxochitl, F. d'Alva—Historia Chichimeca : Relaciones, published by A. Chavero. Mexico, 1891–2.
Kingsborough, Lord—Antiquities of Mexico. London, 1830.
  (The handsome engravings of the pinturas in this vast work
have now been rendered obsolete by the issue of copies of these
manuscripts reproduced by photographic processes. As regards
the letterpress, Lord Kingsborough's attempt to prove a connection between the Aztecs and the lost Ten Tribes of Israel
renders the work one of bibliographical interest only.)
Mendieta, G. de—Historia Ecclesiastica Indiana. Mexico, 1870.
  (Throws some light on manners and customs.)
Nadaillac, Marquis de—Prehistoric America. London, 1885.
  (Contains a considerable amount of matter relating to Mexican
antiquities, but the author's theories on the subject display no
prolonged acquaintance with the study, which was somewhat out
out of his line as a prehistoric archæologist.)
Orozco y Berra—Geographia de las lenguas y carta etnografica de
  Mexico. Mexico, 1864.
  (Invaluable for Mexican ethnology and geographical distri-
bution.)

Payne, E. J.—History of the New World called America.
(A work of profound insight and patient research.)
Peñafiel, A.—Monumentas del Arte Mexicano Antiguo. Berlin,
1890.
(Valuable for reproductions of the pinturas.)
Pimentel, Francesco—Lenguas Indigenas de Mexico. Mexico, 1865.
Prescott, W. H.—History of the Conquest of Mexico. Boston,
1843.
(The result of some two years' study only.)
Sahagun, Bernardino—Historia General de las Cosas de Nueva
España. Mexico, 1829.
Starr, F.—The Indians of Southern Mexico. Chicago, 1899.
Tezozomoc, F. de A.—Chronica Mexicana (in Kingsborough,
Vol. IX).
Thomas, Cyrus, and Magee, W. J.—The History of North America.
Philadelphia, 1908.
(A scholarly and invaluable work.)
Torquemada, Juan de—Monarchia Indiana. Madrid, 1723.
Tylor, E. B.—Anahuac. London, 1861.
(An interesting volume of travels and archæological observa-
tions in Mexico.)
Vetancurt, A. de—Teatro Mexicano. Mexico, 1697-98.
Veytia, M.—Historia Antigua de Mejico. Mexico, 1836.
(Valuable for the early antiquities of the Nahua.)
Wilson, Daniel—Prehistoric Man. London, 1876.
(Deals with American archæology as a whole, with numerous
references to Mexico. Somewhat obsolete.)
Zurita, A. de—Rapports sur les différentes classes des chefs de
la Nouvelle Espagne. (In Ternaux-Compans' collection of
Travels, Vol. II. Series II.)
(Invaluable for the study of Aztec laws.)
Bulletin 28 of the Bureau of American Ethnology contains trans-
lations of valuable essays on Mexican antiquities by the
German scholars Förstemann, Seler, Schellhas, etc.

NOTE ON THE MEXICAN LANGUAGE.

Like all American languages the Mexican or Nahuan tongue is "incorporative." This term implies that several ideas are incorporated or welded into one word. A few examples may assist this definition. The word tlatocatecpanchantzinco means "revered-house-of-the-sovereign-family," and quinextiquiuh is the equivalent for "he-should-spy-out-for-them." In these compound words we have parts, or in cases the whole, of certain words so intimately welded into one expression that they lose their individuality and become merely portions of the whole. The complete form of the name Montezuma or Motecuhzoma Moteuczomaithuicamina, implies "when-the-chief-is-angry-he-shoots-to-heaven," and is a good example of the "incorporated" or welded word.

INDEX

THE PRONUNCIATION OF MEXICAN

The only difficulty presented by the pronunciation of Mexican proper names is the sounding of the letter "*x*," which is pronounced as "*sh*," in most instances, especially before a consonant. Before a vowel, on the other hand, it usually retains its English sound. Thus in Mexico, the *x*-sound is retained, whilst in the name Ixtlilxochitl (pronounced Ishtlilshotshitl) it will be seen that the *x* preceding the *t* becomes soft, and that the *ch* is pronounced *tsh* for reasons of euphony. The "*tl*" sound which occurs with such frequency in Mexican is almost a click of the tongue, and is really unpronounceable by Europeans. The vowel-sounds are pronounced as in French or Italian.

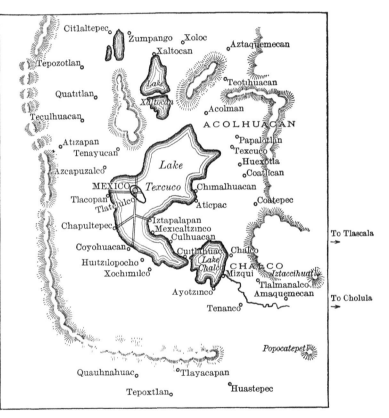

Map of the Valley of Mexico.

www.ingramcontent.com/pod-product-compliance
Ingram Content Group UK Ltd.
Pitfield, Milton Keynes, MK11 3LW, UK
UKHW042146280225
455719UK00001B/144